ar Energy and

s in Tourism

# obal Issues 1

Eileen Armstrong and
Stephen Roulston

**Colourpoint
Educational**

Rewarding Learning

## A2 LEVEL

© Eileen Armstrong, Stephen Roulston and Colourpoint Books 2010

ISBN: 978 1 906578 57 2

First Edition
First Impression

Layout and design: April Sky Design
Printed by: GPS Colour Graphics Ltd

**Colourpoint Books**
Colourpoint House
Jubilee Business Park
21 Jubilee Road
Newtownards
County Down
Northern Ireland
BT23 4YH

Tel:  028 9182 6339
Fax: 028 9182 1900
E-mail: info@colourpoint.co.uk
Web site: www.colourpointeducational.com

## The Authors

**Eileen Armstrong** has a B.A. (Hons) in Geography from QUB. She began her teaching career in St Dominic's Grammar School, Belfast and is currently teaching in Sullivan Upper School, Holywood. In addition she has widespread experience with CCEA as an examiner. She became Principal Examiner for A-level Human Geography in 1996 and was a co-writer of the current AS and A2 level specification.

The author would like to thank the following people who supplied photographs for this book: Professor Steven Royle (QUB), Gregory Armstrong, Rachel Irwin (Colourpoint Books). The author would also like to acknowledge the help and support of her family and colleagues at Sullivan Upper School, Holywood.

**Stephen Roulston** began his teaching career in Foyle and Londonderry College, teaching there briefly before moving to Ballymena Academy, where he became Head of Geography. After a spell as Geography Field Officer with NEELB, he joined C2k as a Curriculum Consultant. In 2010 he became the lecturer for PGCE Geography at the University of Ulster. He has wide experience in examining, currently as a Principal Examiner at A-level.

The author would like to acknowledge the invaluable help from Colourpoint Books, comments on an early draft from Jenny Proudfoot and also the support of his family.

# Contents

**Introduction**

Introduction to Global Issues . . . . . . . . . . . . . . . . . . . . . . . . . . . . . . . . . . 6

**Nuclear Energy**

What is Nuclear Energy? . . . . . . . . . . . . . . . . . . . . . . . . . . . . . . . . . . . 10
The Uses of Nuclear Energy . . . . . . . . . . . . . . . . . . . . . . . . . . . . . . . . 12
The Issues and Impacts of Nuclear Energy . . . . . . . . . . . . . . . . . . . . 14
The Nuclear Debate . . . . . . . . . . . . . . . . . . . . . . . . . . . . . . . . . . . . . 34
Primary Investigation . . . . . . . . . . . . . . . . . . . . . . . . . . . . . . . . . . . . 38

**Issues in Tourism**

The Changing Nature and Characteristics of Tourism. . . . . . . . . . . . . . 42
The Consequences of Tourism Change . . . . . . . . . . . . . . . . . . . . . . . 49
Ecotourism . . . . . . . . . . . . . . . . . . . . . . . . . . . . . . . . . . . . . . . . . . . 62
Primary Investigation . . . . . . . . . . . . . . . . . . . . . . . . . . . . . . . . . . . . 71

**Glossary**

Nuclear Energy . . . . . . . . . . . . . . . . . . . . . . . . . . . . . . . . . . . . . . . . 76
Issues in Tourism . . . . . . . . . . . . . . . . . . . . . . . . . . . . . . . . . . . . . . . 79

# INTRODUCTION

## Introduction to Global Issues

Geography is primarily concerned with issues. These can be related to any aspect of Geography, including destruction of coral reefs, climate change, growth of settlements, new transport developments, population relocation and so on. This is why a good newspaper is full of Geography. An article on the causes and impact of flooding in the UK on one page could be followed by one on the Occupied Territories of Palestine. It is also why Geography is the relevant subject in today's world, informing both the decision-makers and the general public, and providing them with the skills and understanding needed to make sense of a complex world.

In the CCEA A2 Specification there is a section on Global Issues. It provides an opportunity to investigate global issues and debates related to our sustainable future. You will study one of four elements, two of which (Nuclear Energy and Issues in Tourism) are covered in this book. Whichever topic you cover, you will have an opportunity to:

- Conduct fieldwork using primary collection techniques.
- Develop an understanding and awareness of sustainability.
- Understand the need for sustainable solutions to the consequences of modern living.
- Appreciate that there are different opinions, attitudes and values in relation to issues.
- Recognise that compromise is needed to address Geographical issues.
- Appreciate that development of economic resources has environmental consequences that need to be managed with care.

This book aims to provide you with the information you need to prepare you for the topic you are covering, and it provides a range of websites to develop further awareness of the issue. Researching these and other sources will bring an even fuller and deeper understanding of the issue. Remember that issues are controversial – you may have views which differ from those of your fellow candidates. One of the ways to enhance your understanding of these issues is to debate them, to disagree about them, to challenge the views of others and to challenge your own views. Understanding that other views on a topic may differ from your own but remain valid is an important consequence of this element of your A2 course and learning to compromise will be an important outcome.

### Fieldwork

Studying your selected element (Nuclear Energy or Issues in Tourism) will provide an opportunity to engage in a small piece of fieldwork in which you can gather primary data. This is data that you find for yourself, rather than using data that someone else has gathered and summarised in a textbook, website or other source. The learning outcomes for each of the two elements are shown below.

| Element | Learning Outcome |
|---|---|
| Nuclear Energy | Use primary data collection techniques to investigate local attitudes/issues relating to nuclear energy. |
| Issues in Tourism | Use primary data collection techniques to investigate aspects of tourism and its management. |

You are free to identify issues or attitudes appropriate to your locality. For the element of Nuclear Energy, for example, you could look at local attitudes to nuclear energy generation; should there be more nuclear power generated, and, if so, would you be happy to have a nuclear power station sited near you in Northern Ireland? If studying Issues in Tourism you could look at the impact of hill walking in an area near you or the impact of day trippers to a resort or other attraction. Managing tourism in an area will also give many opportunities for study. This is an opportunity to choose an issue which is local and current, or a non-local issue which resonates with the people in the local area and about which they are likely to have views.

## Stages of a Fieldwork Investigation

A geographical investigation consists of a number of stages which have to be followed if the experience is to be logical and meaningful. These are the same stages as you followed for your AS fieldwork and are standard to all the fieldwork you have done in Geography.

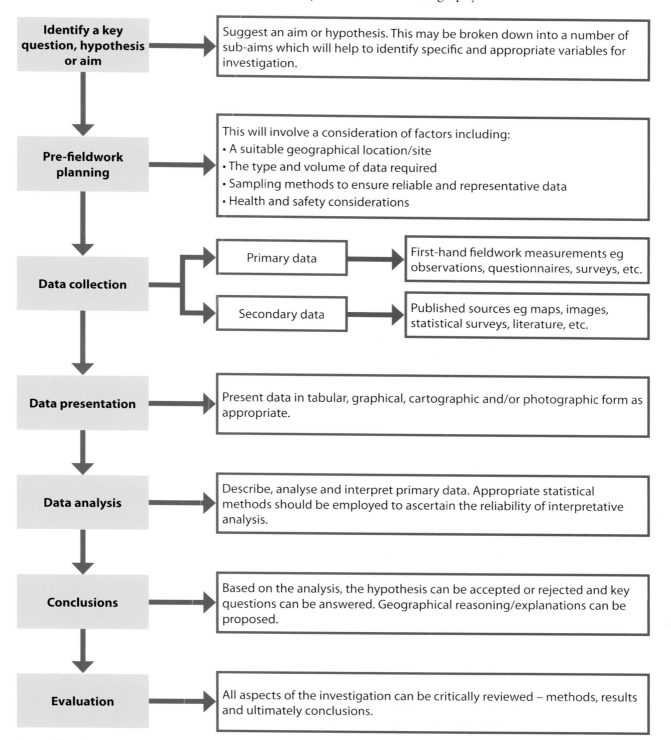

Source: GCE Teacher Guidance, Geography A2 1 Human Geography and Global Issues, Section B Global Issues (2009): Guidance on the Delivery of Fieldwork at A2, CCEA, 2009

Details on how to engage in a fieldwork investigation, including using sampling techniques and statistical analysis appropriate to the CCEA A Level Specification, can be found in *Skills, Techniques and Decision Making*, (Colourpoint, 2008).

## Examining the Fieldwork Investigation

There will be one question set for each global issue on the Global Issues paper each year. Each question will have a number of subsections, one of which will focus on the fieldwork. Candidates may be asked questions related to each stage of the fieldwork process:

- Planning
- Choice of site/location
- Sampling methods chosen (or decision not to sample as appropriate)
- Health and safety considerations
- Data collection
- Data collection techniques
- Choice of secondary data (if appropriate)
- Data presentation
- Identification and justification of data presentation techniques for data collected (note: candidates will not be expected to produce table of data, graphs or maps in the examination)
- Data analysis and interpretation
- An outline of their main findings supported by appropriate geographical explanation
- Conclusion(s) drawn in the light of the aim and or hypothesis/hypotheses
- Evaluation
- Critical review of all aspects of the investigation – methods, results and conclusions

*Source: GCE Teacher Guidance, Geography A2 1 Human Geography and Global Issues, Section B Global Issues (2009): Guidance on the Delivery of Fieldwork at A2, CCEA, 2009*

You should visit the CCEA website (www.ccea.org.uk) to get the most up-to-date information regarding the assessment of this component of the A2 examination.

# NUCLEAR ENERGY

# WHAT IS NUCLEAR ENERGY?

All matter is made up of atoms. **Nuclear energy** is power produced from controlled nuclear reactions. These reactions are caused when two nuclei or nuclear particles are made to collide and, as a result, generate large amounts of heat. The nuclear reaction in which the nucleus of an atom splits into smaller parts is called nuclear **fission**. In controlled reactions, the result is non-explosive. Atoms of heavy elements such as uranium, thorium, and plutonium are used to produce nuclear energy. These naturally occurring elements are not in themselves hazardous. However, after nuclear reactions have occurred, the material is radioactive and potentially dangerous.

There is an alternative technology based around nuclear **fusion**. This is when multiple atomic nuclei join together producing a release of energy. This is the process that is happening in our sun and other stars. Fusion reactions are believed to be safer than fission and have been achieved, although only on a small scale. Nuclear scientists continue to experiment on producing fusion reactions. Many believe that fusion is a very promising energy source for the future as a result of the short-lived radioactivity of the produced waste and the low carbon emissions. However, so far scientists have not managed to develop fusion technology on a large scale.

**Resource 1**     *Nuclear power plant in Cattenom, France*

Commercial nuclear plants use nuclear fission reactions and turn the heat produced into electricity. The energy produced heats water into steam, which is used to generate electricity in a turbine. A model of nuclear power generation can be viewed in the early stages of the nuclear power station simulation, on the ESA21 website: http://esa21.kennesaw.edu/activities/nukeenergy/nuke.htm

In 2007, 14% of all the electricity produced in the world came from nuclear power plants. Some countries have a much higher percentage than this with France, for example, getting 76.2% of its electricity from nuclear plants. At the same time Belgium, Sweden and Germany are currently closing reactors under pressure of public opinion. In 1987 the Italian people voted in a referendum to phase out nuclear power. The Italian government overturned this in July 2009, allowing the immediate resumption of an Italian nuclear programme. Among countries currently building new plants, or considering doing so, are the USA, Japan, Russia, India and China. The UK currently have plans for 10 new plants in England and Wales.

Of course nuclear energy is more than just the provision of electricity. There are also nuclear weapons and health considerations associated with the use of nuclear energy, and these too will be dealt with here.

### Half-lives and measures of radioactivity: let's get the hard stuff out of the way

Radioactivity arises naturally from the decay of particular forms of some elements, called isotopes. Some isotopes are radioactive, however, most are not. The half-life is the time it takes for a radioactive isotope (sometimes called a radioisotope) to lose half of its radioactivity. Four half-lives reduces the radioactivity to 1/16 of the original radioactivity and eight half-lives reduces it to 1/256. The half-life of caesium-137 is just over 30 years, so it would take 120 years for caesium-137 to drop its radioactivity to 1/16 of its original level.

Becquerel (Bq) is a measure of the rate of radioactive decay. One Bq is the same as one atomic disintegration per second. Becquerels can indicate the activity of all the radioactive elements in a place or sample or, more commonly, for a particular radioactive element such as caesium-137. Curies (Ci) are also used as a measure of radiation. One Curie is the equivalent of 37,000,000,000 or $3.7^{10}$ Becquerels.

The dose of radiation absorbed by an organ or tissue is measured by the unit Sievert (Sv). As this is a very large unit the milli Sievert (mSv), one thousandth of a Sievert, is often used. Everyone is constantly exposed to natural radiation which comes from uranium in the earth's crust, radiation from outer space, from various naturally radioactive materials in the diet and from radon gas in the air. In the UK the average natural dose per person is 2.2 mSv, but in Cornwall the granite rock increases that to 6 mSv. A return flight from Belfast to London would increase an individual's dose by about 0.01 mSv as a result of additional radiation from space. The International Commission on Radiological Protection recommends a dose limit at 1 mSv, excluding natural and medical sources.

# THE USES OF NUCLEAR ENERGY

**Resource 2** — *A Russian nuclear-powered ballistic missile submarine*

Nuclear energy has a wide range of uses. It can be used to generate electricity, as we have seen, but that same energy can also be harnessed for other uses, for example, to power submarines. Nuclear submarines have an onboard nuclear power reactor and, as these don't need air to produce electricity, the submarine can operate for long periods without surfacing. The power produced is also considerable and modern nuclear submarines do not need refueled during their 25 year lifetime.

Nuclear technology also confers some benefits to health, in terms of prevention, diagnosis and treatment.

### 1. Prevention

Many hospital supplies are subjected to radiation to ensure that all bacteria, viruses and all other living organisms that might be harmful are eliminated. Surgical masks, dressings, syringes and so on are made sterile in this way. As the radiation used is a cold process, plastics or other heat-sensitive materials can be sterilised. More than 40% of all single-use medical supplies are treated in this way.

### 2. Diagnosis

Minute quantities of radioisotopes have been used since the 1950s to help in the diagnosis of medical conditions, as they are easy to detect and measure using special cameras. There are now over 100 uses for isotopes in medical diagnosis and millions of diagnostic procedures are undertaken each year using them. For example, they can tell how effectively an organ is functioning, how well the body is absorbing various substances, where tumours are located and their size. Their use often eliminates the need for invasive exploratory surgery.

### 3. Treatment

Paradoxically, given the link to cancer formation by radiation, it can also be used to treat diseases, especially cancer. An external beam of radiation can be aimed at a cancerous tumour to remove it (**Resource 3**). Other treatments include the insertion of radioactive sources into or adjacent to tumours to kill the cancerous cells. New treatments using radioisotopes attached to antibodies offer hope in the treatment of diseases such as liver cancer, brain cancer and non-Hodgkin's lymphoma. The antibodies seek out the cancer cells and connect to them. The radiation dose will then be very effectively targeted at the cancerous cells.

In More Economically Developed Countries (MEDCs), about one half of the population will rely on what is termed nuclear medicine at some stage in their lives.

Radioisotopes can be used in agriculture to combat disease and to help to produce weather resistant crops. A further use is in the preservation of food. They are also used in the home and in industry. For example, the most common home smoke detectors use an ionisation chamber containing a very tiny amount of americium, a radioisotope derived from plutonium formed in a nuclear reactor.

*A man receiving electron radiation therapy for skin cancer*   **Resource 3**

## Health issues

There are a number of health effects as radiation affects living cells. At low radiation levels the biological changes are small and may be able to be repaired by the body. While living cells may have their DNA (the genetic structure of the cell) damaged, some such damage may be repaired by the body. Other damage may occur to the DNA and the cell may die, which means that the damage is not passed on. If a cell's DNA is mutated but the cell does not die, that may pass on the mutated DNA to other cells as it divides, which may contribute to cancer. In extreme cases, irreparable DNA damage occurs, which produces premature aging and cancer. Some of the damage to the DNA can be passed on to children, even if they were not subject to the radiation dose, causing malformations and disease in the next generation.

Exposure to radiation over a long period of time is called chronic exposure. We are exposed to radiation from a range of natural sources all the time and it is difficult to study the effects of chronic exposure as variations in the source of those natural radiation sources: rock type, number of flights taken and so on will vary from individual to individual.

Exposure to acute radiation occurs during a short period of time and is more easily studied. Much of what we know about this came from studies of the nuclear explosions at Hiroshima and Nagasaki in 1945. Cancers associated with such high level radiation include leukaemia (cancer of the bone marrow) and cancers of the thyroid, bladder, breast, lung, colon, liver, oesophagus, ovarian, skin and stomach.

There is a delay between the radiation dose and the cancer formation. As a result it is often difficult to prove a link between the two as the same cancers can be caused by smoking, alcohol use or poor diet, for example. Nevertheless, the link between cancer and high doses of radiation is clear. At lower doses, below 10 mSv for example, it is much harder to gauge the risk. However, it is almost certain that people with exposure to radiation at this level face an increased risk of developing leukaemia or other cancers. Some work would suggest that any dose, no matter how small, increases the risk.

**Exercise**

1. **Question from CCEA January 2010**

   Briefly describe one of the following applications of nuclear energy:

   • power generation;

   • medical uses.      (4)

2. **Question from CCEA Specimen Paper 2010**

   Discuss one way in which nuclear energy can be said to benefit humanity.   (4)

# THE ISSUES AND IMPACTS OF NUCLEAR ENERGY

## Radioactive contamination

It is clear that nuclear technology can bring many benefits to the human race. Perhaps the main one will come to be the ability to create power while not contributing to climate-changing emissions to the atmosphere. However, it is impossible to discuss issues around nuclear energy without considering the potential for accidents and the most serious nuclear accident so far.

A nuclear power complex in what was then the Union of Soviet Socialist Republics (USSR), and now part of Ukraine, called **Chernobyl**, is notorious as the site of the world's largest nuclear accident. Located 85 km north of Kiev, and close to what is now the border with Belarus, the site had four nuclear reactors. The area around the complex was heavily wooded and with a relatively low population density. However, there was a new city close by, Pripyat, built to serve the complex. At just 3 km away from the Chernobyl complex, it had 49,000 inhabitants. The old town of Chernobyl, with a population of about 12,500, was 15 km away. In all, about 120,000 people lived within a 30 km radius of the Chernobyl nuclear site.

## The accident

On the night of 25/26 April 1986, a test was performed on Reactor Number 4 in the Chernobyl complex. The test was designed to see whether the turbines could produce enough energy to keep coolant pumps running to give time for an emergency diesel generator to be started, should there have been a loss of power. This required the reactor to be powered down to 25% of its usual capacity. In order to ensure that the test would not be interrupted, the safety systems in the reactor were deliberately switched off.

The test did not go according to plan. The reactor power level fell to less than 1% for reasons which are not entirely clear. As the crew slowly increased the power level there was an unexpected surge of power. An emergency shutdown, which should have stopped the chain reaction, failed. Almost immediately, the power level and the temperature rose steeply and the crew lost control of the reactor. A violent explosion occurred and the 1,000 tonne sealing cap on the reactor was destroyed exposing the reactor core. The fuel rods melted as temperatures reached over 2,000 degrees Celsius. Radioactive materials were blasted up into the atmosphere and a plume of radioactive material was carried upwards (**Resource 4**).

The reasons for the accident are not certain, partly because those running the test died, but are likely to have been a combination of poor reactor design and human error.

**Resource 4** *The nuclear reactor at Chernobyl*

## Management of the disaster

Firefighters were soon on the scene to try to extinguish the fire and stop the radioactive plume that the fire was carrying up into the atmosphere. Water was pumped into the core of the reactor for ten hours following the accident but it proved impossible to extinguish the main fire. From 27 April until 5 May military helicopters dumped 2,400 tonnes of lead and 1,800 tonnes of sand in an effort to smother the fire. This actually had the effect of increasing the heat below the dumped materials, leading to even more radiation emissions. The explosion and fire threw particles of the nuclear fuel and dangerous radioactive elements into the air and residents in the surrounding areas commented on the radioactive cloud. By 6 May the fire in Reactor Number 4 was under control and was finally extinguished on 10 May.

The firefighters were not told how dangerously radioactive the smoke and debris were and they may not even have been told that the fire was not a standard electrical fire. The commander of the first crew on the scene died of acute radiation poisoning on 9 May. All of the 600 firefighters and the crew who were operating the plant were most severely affected by radiation. What radiation levels they were subjected to are not known as the instruments available could not read such high levels, but it is likely that some people got fatal doses of radiation within a few minutes. In the UK, the maximum dose of radiation for the general public should not exceed 1 millisievert (mSv) per year. 134 of the firefighters and crew received doses of up to 13 sieverts (Sv) – 13,000 times the safe annual dose – in just a few hours. 28 of the firefighters and crew of the plant died shortly afterwards.

In all 800,000 people were involved in the clean up operations around Chernobyl and many have suffered from health problems since. It is thought that 300,000 may have received more than 500 mSv of radiation. The number of deaths of this group that can be attributed to the radiation is hotly disputed, but some estimates put it at 25,000 so far.

## The local population

The city of Pripyat was not immediately evacuated as the USSR authorities tried to conceal the scale of the disaster. However, on 27 April, 36 hours after the accident, all 49,000 inhabitants of the city were evacuated. To reduce baggage, the inhabitants were told that the evacuation was temporary and many personal items still remain in the city, although it remains uninhabitable. Within 10 days, 130,000 people living around the reactor were evacuated.

*View of the abandoned city of Pripyat, with the Chernobyl plant in the background*

**Resource 5**

From the beginning of May, levels of radioactivity in milk and drinking water were monitored in the affected areas and, on 23 May, iodine was distributed to prevent the absorption of some of the radioactivity in the thyroid gland. However, as most radioactivity was released in the first 10 days after the explosion, this may have been too late for many people.

The whole area is now an exclusion zone and people are not allowed to visit it without special permission from the government (**Resource 5**).

**Resource 6**    *Location of Chernobyl in the Ukraine*

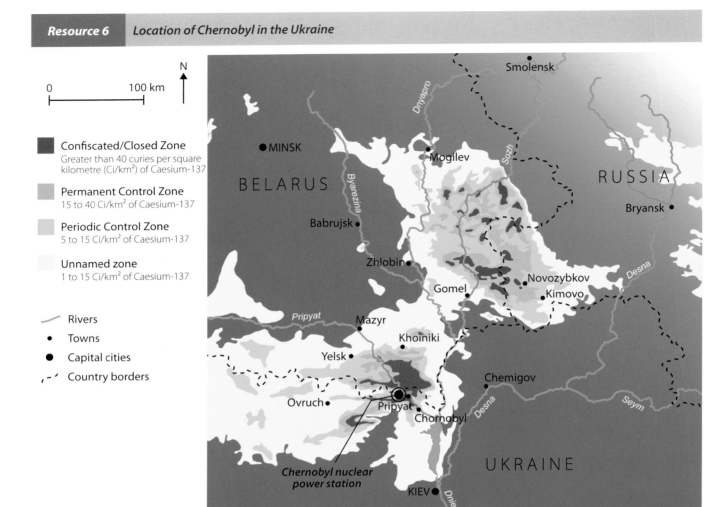

## Countries affected

The areas with the highest levels of contamination are in the north of Ukraine, the south and east of Belarus and the Russian area bordering Belarus (**Resource 6**). Estimates suggest that between 125,000 and 146,000 km² of the three countries are heavily contaminated with caesium-137. At the time of the accident there were about 7 million inhabitants of that area and about a quarter of a million have now been resettled or have left the area themselves. However, the remainder of the population, including 1,000,000 children, continues to live in contaminated areas.

## How much contamination was there?

The most widely distributed radioactive element in the contaminated area is caesium-137, which has a half life of 30 years. This is the reason why maps usually show this element as contamination per square kilometre in Becquerels or in Curies (**Resource 7**). Measured using a Geiger counter, one Becquerel is the equivalent of one radioactive disintegration each second. The contamination spread over a large part of Western Europe, although it tended to concentrate close to the explosion and in higher land elsewhere, where there tended to be more precipitation (**Resource 7**).

## Closing the reactor

Seven months after the accident, the reactor building was enclosed in a reinforced concrete casing, nicknamed a sarcophagus after the ancient Egyptian coffins. An interim measure, with an expected lifespan of 20 to 30 years, this was designed to absorb the radiation and contain the molten core. While it has been moderately successful in that, it was built in haste. As it is supported by the damaged remains of the reactor building, there is a fear that the structure will become unstable.

In 1997, the G7 countries (Canada, France, Germany, Italy, Japan, UK, and USA) with Russia, the EU and Ukraine launched a plan to confine the radioactivity in Chernobyl Reactor No 4 for the next 100 years. A steel sliding arched structure, called New Safe Confinement (NSC), will be constructed 450 m west of the destroyed reactor. At 190 m wide and 200 m long, it is said that it will be the largest moveable structure ever built. Constructed by a French firm, the NSC will be moved along greased steel plates to cover the existing structure. The present unstable 'sarcophagus' will then be painstakingly removed using robotised cranes and where possible human workers wearing appropriate protective clothing. This will involve the dismantling and removal of the concrete roof of the present structure, parts of the original reactor structure, the accident debris and a number of large beams which were used in the construction of the first protective structure. Only after that has happened can the task begin to remove the nuclear fuel. Before this can be done a deep geological repository must be constructed in Ukraine, or disposal casks designed and temporary storage identified and built. The reported completion date for the NSC is 2012. More information on this plan is available from the BBC website: http://news.bbc.co.uk/1/hi/6999140.stm

The accident has had widespread effects on the area around Chernobyl as result of **radioactive contamination**. This is the uncontrolled distribution of radioactive material in an area. **Resource 7** shows that levels of radioactive contamination of caesium-137 were very high, particularly close to the scene of the explosion and in what are now the countries of Belarus, Ukraine and the Russian Federation. Excessive levels of radioactive contamination can be very

**Contamination of caesium-137 resulting from the Chernobyl explosion**                    **Resource 7**

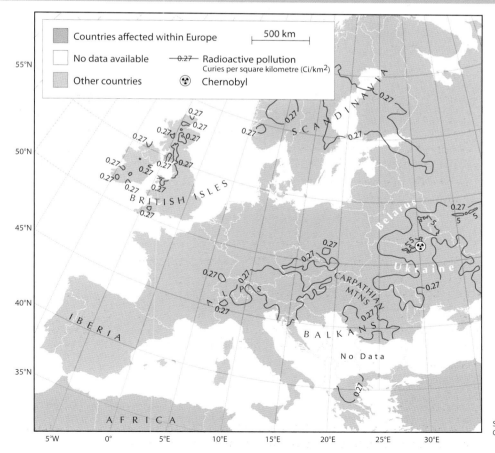

Source: Resource for CCEA January 2009

dangerous, posing a major threat to environments and to people.

In terms of people the radioactivity is harmful if it is eaten, inhaled or absorbed through the skin. The effects of contamination are the same as being exposed to other forms of radiation such as x-rays. Some radioisotopes may target specific organs increasing the chances of cancers there. For example, the Chernobyl disaster in Ukraine produced large volumes of radioactive iodine. The thyroid gland in humans controls how quickly the body burns energy and, among other functions, takes up most of the iodine in the body. Milk taken from animals which have eaten contaminated grass may contain the radioactive iodine and, once drunk, may contribute to cancers being formed, especially of the thyroid gland. Additionally people may eat plants or drink water which has been contaminated.

## Impact on the environment

### 1. Soil

The radioactivity carried from the scene of the explosion fell to the ground and contaminated the soil. Apart from how much radioactivity fell in a place, how badly the soil became contaminated depended on many factors: the natural decay in the radioactivity, the type of soil and how the radioactive elements move in the earth. Belarus received 70% of the fallout from Chernobyl and 22% of the country was contaminated with caesium-137. It is estimated that 16% will still be contaminated in 2016.

Where caesium-137 has been deposited in the soil, it will generally persist for years in the top five centimetres of the topsoil. This is exactly where many plants have their roots. The coniferous forests which are so common in many of the contaminated areas are particularly susceptible to radiation as the roots and leaf litter retain the radiation. As needles fall the radiation contained on them accumulates further.

In areas with clay soils, caesium-137 is not easily washed downwards and will tend to be retained in the top five centimetres. Strontium-90 is a soluble element so is more easily washed out of the soil. Up to 80% of it has already been dissolved in the groundwater and from there has entered the rivers and lakes of the area. Traces of strontium have been found in fields in southern Ukraine which were irrigated with water from the River Dnieper. This river has, as a tributary, the Pripyat, which is the river next to the Chernobyl plant (**Resource 5**) and gave its name to the city.

Excavating the contaminated soil and replacing it with non-contaminated soil is not economically viable, except on a small scale, such as beside schools.

### 2. Water and air

Radiation on the surface of the rivers, particularly the Pripyat and Dniepr, transported the contamination over a wide area. Protective dams were built to slow the spread of the radiation but could not halt it altogether. Radioactivity still continues to leach into the rivers, particularly during flooding, increasing risks of exposure to radiation for the 30 million people who rely on the Dnieper basin for drinking water.

Groundwater is contaminated with radioactive elements, particularly strontium and most of the rural population depends on wells for their drinking water. Even more worrying is another radioactive contaminant, americium, a decay product of plutonium which can migrate into ground water more quickly than plutonium. As americium has a half-life of 433 years, the water will be contaminated for a considerable time.

### 3. Plants and animals

In all there was radioactive contamination of 18,000 km² of agricultural land and 2640 km² of this is now too contaminated to be farmed. Forests were also badly contaminated with, in the Ukraine alone, over 40% of the forest in the country being affected.

Forest plants such as mushrooms, ferns and grasses have a high accumulation of radioactivity and it is also found in the berries of the plants which grow there. Studies are continuing, but there is some evidence of genetic mutations in some of the plants and a reduction in germination rates in the heavily contaminated areas.

Recent studies have shown that the numbers of small insects such as bumblebees, butterflies, grasshoppers, dragonflies and spiders around the nuclear power complex reduced after the accident. As the ecosystem relies on such insects to germinate plants and to act as a food source for other organisms in the food chain, it is likely that other parts of the ecosystem are also affected. A sample of barn swallows examined around the site of the Chernobyl explosion between 1991 and 2006 were found to have more physical abnormalities than swallows studied elsewhere in Europe. Encouragingly, as the abnormal birds mated less frequently than normal birds, the percentage of young inheriting the defects was low, and the abnormalities seem to be evolving out rapidly. More information on the wildlife surrounding Chernobyl is available from the BBC website: http://news.bbc.co.uk/1/hi/sci/tech/7949314.stm

Studies of wildlife are made more complicated because of the absence of people around Chernobyl. Some research even seems to suggest that wildlife is thriving in the area.

Domestic herbivores, such as cattle and goats, accumulate radioactivity as they feed on contaminated plants and this can be passed on in milk and meat. In places where cattle are farmed as part of the forest system, as in Belarus, those animals are particularly badly affected.

Wild carnivores, such as wolves and foxes, have accumulated even higher levels of radioactivity than herbivores, with some estimates suggesting that they are up to 12 times more contaminated than herbivores, as the radioactivity of their prey accumulates in their bodies.

Rivers and lakes were badly affected with radioactive contamination and often these elements have concentrated in the sediments. With concentrations of up to 1 million Bq per cubic metre of sediment reported in Belarus, bottom feeding fish such as carp can be very heavily contaminated.

## Impact on people and the economy

### 1. Food supplies

With grasses highly contaminated in places, this has an impact on grazing livestock. Feeding them uncontaminated hay or feed additives can reduce the contamination of meat and milk, and the Ukrainian government, for example, distributes feed additives to all farmers free of charge.

There are many subsistence farmers in Belarus, Ukraine and the Russian Federation who rely on producing their own food and they are particularly badly affected as little of what they consume is brought in from uncontaminated areas.

The governments have had to impose stringent regulations regarding levels of contamination in food. For example, in 2000, Ukraine performed more than 1 million tests

*Unofficial market in Kiev*    **Resource 8**

The fish for sale in this unofficial market in Kiev could be a source of radiation. Vegetables grown on personal plots alongside mushrooms and berries gathered from the forests may also pose a risk to consumers.

on foodstuffs from state farms destined for sale in markets to ensure that levels of contamination were within safe limits. Food which is grown by individuals or which is gathered in the forests or caught in the rivers or lakes, however, is not subject to such restrictions. In addition, hunting and fishing bans in the affected areas seem not to have been very successful.

It is believed that vegetables grown or livestock raised for home consumption will have contamination between 2 and 5 times the limits set by government. Rural populations are particularly at risk and it is thought that up to 98% of the radiation which rural people receive will be from home-grown food raised in contaminated soil. Also these communities have always supplemented their home production by gathering from the forests and by hunting and fishing. As we have seen the products of the forests and the fish and game tend to be highly contaminated.

### 2. Human health

The impact of the accident on human health has been considerable, although the numbers who have died as a direct consequence of the accident are disputed. It is agreed that, between the date of the explosion and 2002, at least 4,000 children and adolescents in Belarus, Ukraine and Russian Federation have developed thyroid cancer. There is a fear in some quarters that this number will rise very considerably over the coming decades, perhaps reaching 8,000 or more. However, it is not yet clear what the scale will be and one cancer specialist put the probable figure of people with thyroid cancers as high as 100,000. Others produce entirely different figures. The Chernobyl Forum, consisting of the International Atomic Energy Agency, a number of United Nations' organisations and the World Bank, produced much smaller figures of the consequences of the Chernobyl explosion:

- 28 deaths from acute radiation poisoning in the first three months following the accident
- 14 patient deaths from a variety of medical conditions including thyroid cancer, and
- 4,000 deaths estimated from cancers

(Source: Figures from the United Nations Office for the Coordination of Humanitarian Affairs)

These figures can be contrasted with the report commissioned by Greenpeace, an environmental organisation which takes a strong anti-nuclear stance. It concludes that "the most recently published figures indicate that in Belarus, Russia and Ukraine alone, the accident could have resulted in an estimated 200,000 additional deaths in the period between 1990 and 2004". The report has been criticised because it fails to take into account the changes to local health care provision with the break-up of the USSR and the general increases in cancer deaths that this caused.

### 3. The economy

Radioactive contamination from the Chernobyl accident effectively removed a high proportion of the land resource including agriculture, forestry, mineral extraction and factories of affected countries. For example, around one fifth of Belarus' land resource was lost, with 22% of agricultural land and 21% of its forests taken out of production. The total damage to that country has been estimated at US$235 billion. In contrast, the total government spending for 2008 in health, education, road building and so on was estimated at just US$26 billion. Costs related to the Chernobyl explosion made up over 20% of Belarus' spending in the years following the incident and still make up a substantial proportion of all government spending. In Ukraine it is estimated that the economic damage would be US$201 billion up to 2015. Additional Russian expenditure as a consequence of the accident totalled about US$3.8 billion between 1992 and 1998. The costs to their economy would have been considerably more than that.

Some of the other costs to the most affected economies are more difficult to measure but include lost production from the factories located in the contaminated areas. In Belarus, 54 large agricultural and forestry operations and 9 industrial plants had to close. Additionally, 22 sources of raw materials had to cease production. The figures for Ukraine are similar.

Those enterprises that can stay open in the contaminated areas where people are still allowed to live find it difficult to recruit and retain staff, as the young and well-qualified tend to move elsewhere. It also proves difficult to interest investors to stimulate new enterprises in such areas.

The money spent by the governments differed from country to country. Belarus concentrated at first on resettlement grants and developing infrastructure for the resettled people. By 1996, 131,000 people had been resettled from the most contaminated parts of Belarus, with almost 65,000 houses and flats built to accommodate these people. Most of the money now is spent on medical and social aid programmes. Ukraine and Russia from the start focused on social benefits for the affected population. The benefits included free or heavily subsidised medical care, free meals for children and students, monthly allowances and the right to a free 'health holiday' month each year. In Ukraine, the government funded between 400,000 and 500,000 holidays every year between 1994 and 2000.

Many of the investment programmes proved hard to sustain and funding has steadily declined over time. Some projects have left half-built houses and blocks of flats in resettlement villages. The number of people claiming benefits as a consequence of Chernobyl rose steadily over time. In Ukraine, for example, those designated as permanently disabled as a consequence of Chernobyl rose from just 200 in 1991 to over 90,000 in 2001. This may have been related more to the economic crisis of the 1990s, rather than to increasing health difficulties emerging. For some, the benefits became their sole income and their only way of accessing health care. This has produced an unsustainable burden on the governments involved and the spending is being spread more and more thinly. In order to improve the situation in Belarus, benefits there are not now paid to individuals but given to the regional government to spend on medical and social facilities for the affected population.

## 4. Impact on the demographic structure of the areas affected

In Belarus and Russia, all those living in areas with the very highest contamination, with more than 40 Curies per km$^2$ – Ci/km$^2$ (**Resource 6**), were required to leave their homes. In Ukraine the limit was placed lower at 15 Ci/km$^2$, and people living in those areas had to relocate. Some elderly people who did not want to leave their ancestral villages either stayed behind or returned without permission. Residents where there was more than 5 Ci/km$^2$ of caesium-137 had the right to resettlement, but could remain in their homes if they wanted. With 350,400 people resettled in all, this has had a massive impact on Belarus, Russia and Ukraine. Young families with children were the most common group choosing to leave, and this has had an impact on demographic structure in the affected areas. The birth rates are dropping there as the young and productive population has fled. For example, in 1986, prior to the accident, the population of the Gomel District of Belarus was rising by 8% each year. By 2000, the birth rate had dropped from 17.2 per thousand to just 9.7, while mortality rose from 9.2 to 14.8 per thousand. In consequence the population actually declined in 2000.

Having so few young adults is a problem in a number of ways. Companies who require skilled workers find that they cannot get people to do the jobs. There are insufficient doctors and teachers, for example, and in consequence, more people move away from the area. There is also an impact on the areas into which the resettled people are directed, as the social structure of those villages or residential areas of cities changes. The United Nations, which has been closely involved in the settlement programme, has reported tensions between the original inhabitants and the resettled people. The older resettled people find it harder to adapt to living in a new area. There is also a stigma associated with radioactivity, which many of the established population see as an infectious disease. It is also difficult for resettled young people to find a partner, as there is a fear of congenital abnormalities in any children. An additional problem relates to the existing population who are envious of the resettled population's new apartments or houses specially built for them to a higher specification than the original properties. The consequence of all of this is that the resettled population tends not to integrate with their new neighbours but tend to associate almost exclusively with each other. More and more of the resettled population are reported as wishing to return to their original towns and villages, something which will not be possible in most cases.

### 5. Impact on energy supplies

As a result of the Chernobyl accident, Belarus, which was the most severely affected of all countries, has halted its nuclear energy programme. With limited energy resources of its own, Belarus depends very heavily on fuel imports, largely from Russia. A programme had been established in 1992 to encourage efficient use of energy and the development of alternative supplies but progress was hampered because of the cheap gas that Belarus sourced from Russia and there was little impetus to develop alternatives. At this stage Russia subsidised gas to Belarus for $46 per 1,000 m$^2$ (compared to $290 for 1,000 m$^2$ charged to Germany). In 2007, however, the Russian state-owned natural gas supplier Gazprom demanded higher prices. The dispute about fuel pricing escalated until the Russians eventually shut down a pipeline, cutting the supply of oil to Belarus. While this dispute was eventually resolved, Belarus remains vulnerable as a result of its dependence on external suppliers of energy.

In Ukraine, to supplement local sources of coal and the dwindling local supplies of oil and gas, nuclear power was developed. The Chernobyl plant produced nuclear electricity for the first time in 1978. Despite the accident, Ukraine is still committed to having nuclear power as an element of their power generation and have 15 nuclear power stations in operation. However, they also rely on imported natural gas from Russia and price tensions between Ukraine and Russia have resulted in the gas being cut on occasions.

Both of these countries have significant problems with meeting their energy needs and while Ukraine has embraced a strategy that includes nuclear power, Belarus has currently chosen not to continue with that.

## Radioactive contamination in the British Isles

Radioactive contamination as a result of Chernobyl also had an impact on the British Isles, although this was much less than it might have been. It was a summer night with relatively low wind speeds at the time of the accident so radioactive particles were mostly carried up into the upper atmosphere. The winds in that part of the atmosphere dispersed the contamination widely (**Resource 7**) but luckily there was little precipitation in the week following the accident, which would have brought more radioactive particles down to earth in the British Isles.

The main parts of Great Britain (GB) where some rainfall brought the radiation down to earth were in the highlands of North Wales, Cumbria and South-West Scotland. On the island of Ireland, uplands in Northern Ireland, the south Midlands and north-west of the Republic of Ireland were most affected. In all of those places radioactive material (predominantly caesium-137) was deposited. The soil in these areas is predominantly derived from peat and the radioactivity cannot be trapped, allowing plants to take it up easily. In turn this makes the radioactivity gather in animals in the area. While there are wild animals in these areas, there are also large numbers of sheep.

Since the release of the radiation across Europe, the radiation levels in sheep grazing on these upland areas of the UK and Ireland have been monitored. In 1986, almost 9,000 farms and 4 million sheep were affected by the radiation, all in the UK. In Ireland, it was not considered necessary to impose any restriction on the sale or consumption of Irish farm products. However, in some areas of the UK, there are still restrictions in force today on the movement, sale and slaughter of some sheep.

Although all restrictions in Northern Ireland were lifted in 2000, the most recent reports at the time of writing show that some restrictions in GB are being maintained. In the summer of 2008, 5,600 sheep in Cumbria were monitored in six of the nine farms still under restriction. Four of the six farms surveyed had sheep which exceeded permitted contamination levels.

Similar monitoring in Scotland found that the five farms subject to restriction there were still heavily contaminated. Approximately 3,000 sheep there could not be moved, nor could their wool or meat be sold. In North Wales, of the 5,100 farms and two million sheep originally affected, there remain 330 farms and 180,000 sheep under restriction. The most up-to-date report is available from the Food Standards Agency website: http://www.food.gov.uk/science/surveillance/radiosurv/chernobyl/

Chernobyl is not the only source of non-natural radioactive contamination in the British Isles. The nuclear reprocessing plant at Sellafield, on the Irish Sea coast of North-West England, has produced contamination on a number of occasions. In December 2009, for example, a fine of £75,000 was imposed on the owners of Sellafield when two contractors inhaled radioactive contamination when drilling a section of floor. The dust produced and inhaled by the two men was contaminated with plutonium.

Sellafield has also been a focus for Irish government concerns about the Irish Sea and its contamination by radiation. While the Irish Sea has some natural radioactivity, its main source of radioactivity is through liquid discharges from Sellafield. In 2004 the Irish Government welcomed the commitment by the UK Environment Agency, the UK Nuclear Installations Inspectorate and British Nuclear Fuel (BNFL), the company who run the Sellafield operation, to reduce by 90% the discharges of one radioactive element into the Irish Sea. Nevertheless the Irish government continues to press the case. The Irish Department of the Environment, Heritage and Local Government minister, and leader of the Irish Green party, John Gormley, TD, met with his UK equivalent and made it very clear that Ireland continues to have significant concerns about Sellafield and would like it to close. However, another branch of government, the Irish National Food Residue Database, concludes on their website that "The doses incurred by people living in Ireland today as a result of the routine operations at Sellafield are small and do not constitute a significant health risk."

**Sellafield nuclear reprocessing plant**    *Resource 9*

Source: Simon Ledingham

**Resource 10**    *Hiroshima, 6 August 1945*

*Above:* Hiroshima City after the 6 August 1945 atomic bombing.

*Right:* Mushroom cloud from the atomic explosion over Nagasaki on the morning of 9 August 1945. This image was taken from one of the B-29 Superfortresses used in the attack.

**Resource 11**    *Nagasaki, 9 August 1945*

## Nuclear weapons testing

A nuclear weapon is an explosive device which harnesses the vast amounts of energy released by nuclear reactions. They can be relatively small but they have very powerful effects. A modern nuclear weapon weighing around 1,000 kg (imagine 1,000 bags of sugar) has the same explosive power as 1 billion kg of high explosive. A single nuclear weapon of the same size as a conventional bomb, that could be dropped from an aircraft, could destroy a whole city through the force of the blast, and through subsequent fire and radiation.

Only two nuclear weapons have ever been detonated by one country against another. Both of these were dropped on Japan by the USA towards the end of World War II, in 1945. The city of Hiroshima was virtually destroyed (**Resource 10)** and, three days later, the city of Nagasaki suffered the same fate (**Resource 11)**. About 120,000 people, mostly civilian, died immediately and many have died since as a result of radiation.

Since those first bombs were dropped, many more countries have been given or have developed the technology for creating nuclear weapons of their own. Those countries currently in possession of nuclear weapons are known to include the USA, Russia, France, the UK, China, India, Pakistan and North Korea. While Israel officially denies having nuclear weapons, they too are widely believed to possess them. There are estimated to be 27,000 nuclear weapons in the world, belonging to those nine countries. It is said that more than 2,500 of them are still ready to launch at a moment's notice at any time of day on any day of the year. The UK are said to have 160 operational nuclear weapons.

A necessary part of developing and extending nuclear weapon technology involves testing of the weapons. Alternatively they can be exploded to signal political and military strength to potential enemies. Over 2,000 weapon testing events have happened since 1945. Nuclear weapons tests can take place in a range of conditions.

In **atmospheric** testing, the nuclear explosions occur above ground. Usually the nuclear device is placed on a tower or a barge, or is dropped from an aircraft. Any nuclear explosion which takes place close to the earth's surface can pull up debris into a mushroom cloud (**Resource 11**),

*Nuclear weapon test at Bikini Atoll, 1946*

A nuclear weapon test by the United States military at Bikini Atoll, Micronesia, 25 July 1946.

which can increase the volume of radioactive materials falling back to earth – nuclear contamination.

**Underwater** testing happens when nuclear devices are detonated in the sea, usually moored under a ship or barge, and is often designed to see how effective the devices would be against naval military targets. The impact of these tests includes the large amount of radioactive water and steam which is produced (**Resource 12**).

In **underground** testing, nuclear devices are exploded below the earth's surface (**Resource 13**). If tested far enough below the earth's surface, only a very small amount of nuclear contamination may result. However, in more shallow tests, the explosion can burst onto the surface and this will produce a very large amount of radioactive debris on the surface of the earth and extending into the atmosphere.

In 1963, all nuclear and many non-nuclear countries signed up to the Limited Test Ban Treaty. This committed them not to test nuclear weapons in the atmosphere, underwater or in space. However, the treaty did permit underground testing to be carried out. France continued with atmospheric testing until 1974 and China until 1980. The Comprehensive Test Ban Treaty came into force in 1996 and all nuclear testing by these states ceased. Some nuclear testing still goes on by non-signatories to the Comprehensive Test Ban, with a recent test by North Korea in 2009.

As **Resource 14** shows, 1962 was the year when most tests took place, with more than two tests every week on average. During the height of the Cold War between USSR and the USA their tests balance each other, especially after 1970 when USA tests were scaled back.

*Underground testing*

Preparation for an underground nuclear test at the Nevada Test Site in the 1980s. Visible in the photograph are the test monitoring equipment, as well as the subsidence craters created by previous underground nuclear tests.

**Resource 14** *Weapons testing events from 1945 to 1998*

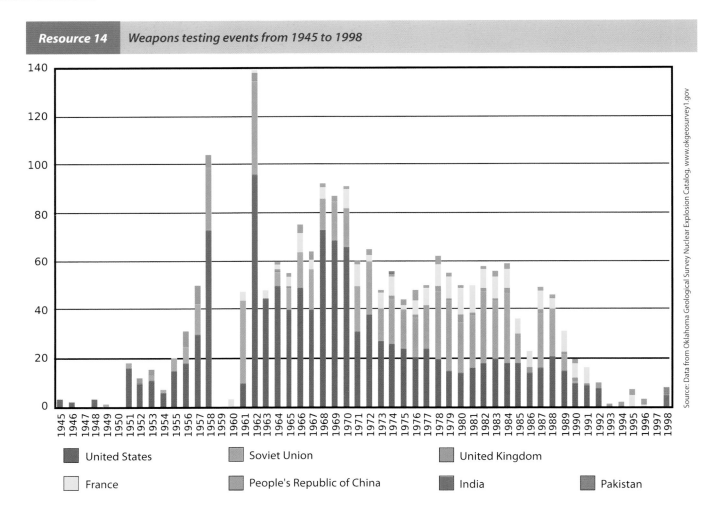

Source: Data from Oklahoma Geological Survey Nuclear Explosion Catalog, www.okgeosurvey1.gov

Legend:
- United States
- Soviet Union
- United Kingdom
- France
- People's Republic of China
- India
- Pakistan

Countries that have developed their nuclear capability in more recent years, such as India and Pakistan, came to testing a little later. However, largely due to the test ban treaties and the lack of proliferation of countries with nuclear weapons, testing is now at a much lower level than it was at its peak.

**Resource 15** *Explosion at Bikini Atoll, 1954*

## The impact of nuclear weapons' testing

Testing nuclear weapons can be hazardous. For example, in 1954 there was a USA atmospheric test on a coral island in the Pacific Ocean, Bikini Atoll (an action that gave us the name of a piece of swimwear then becoming popular). There had been a long history of nuclear testing on this atoll; this test was code-named Castle Bravo.

The explosion produced much more nuclear contamination than had been anticipated and a change in wind direction spread this into areas which had not been cleared in advance of the test. Radioactive material spread over 160 km from Bikini Atoll contaminating a number of populated islands which, while eventually evacuated, had long-lasting effects on the health of the inhabitants. It also affected a Japanese fishing boat, Lucky Dragon No5. Many of the crew became ill and one died as a result of radiation sickness. In addition some of the vessels and staff involved in the testing were also caught out by the unanticipated scale of the explosion and the change in the weather. Many personnel on aircraft carriers, for example, claimed that they had their health impaired by exposure to the radioactive contamination.

Radioactive material was traced to India, Australia and Japan, and there was even a scare about milk contamination in the UK. While the Bikini Atoll test had been organised as a secret military test, it became a major international incident, particularly straining relationships between Japan and the USA. On the positive side, it was also a catalyst in the banning of atmospheric testing of nuclear weapons. A video of the explosion is available on the sonic bomb website: http://www.sonicbomb.com/modules.php?name=Content&pa=showpage&pid =61

As newer countries to the 'nuclear club' developed weapons, they too have tested them. The exception is South Africa, which claims never to have tested its weapons when it had them and has since dismantled its nuclear capability. Some of these more recent tests, just as had happened at Bikini Atoll in 1954, were subject to unexpectedly large explosions and changes in weather. In addition, developments to the technology require ensuring the reliability of new weapons, so some testing is likely to continue. There is a now considerable pressure on countries not to conduct atmospheric tests. In spite of this, leakage from other types of tests is not uncommon.

There has been little compensation for victims of nuclear testing. However, the US government has paid out more than $1.3 billion as a result of the Radiation Exposure Compensation Program of 1990. This covered workers in uranium processing as well as those impacted by testing. Payments were made to both of these groups, who suffered from a range of 27 medical conditions including leukaemia and other cancers. For example, people downwind of the test site in Nevada, in mainland USA, who suffer from any of a number of stated medical conditions, receive $50,000 each. Those who suffer from specific medical conditions and were present at the tests qualify for $75,000. Further information is available from The United States Department of Justice website: http://www.justice.gov/civil/torts/const/reca/about.htm

In Britain, to date, there has been no formal compensation programme for the effects of its testing, which took place mainly in Australia and at Christmas Island in the Pacific Ocean. Despite a concerted and prolonged effort to convince the government that many of those involved in the testing in Christmas Island in the 1950s had suffered adverse health effects as a result of exposure, little progress has been made. Nearly 1,000 survivors of the testing intend to sue the British government in an attempt to secure compensation.

## Nuclear waste

The creation of nuclear energy inevitably involves the production of radioactive waste, sometimes known as **radwaste**. Safe storage and disposal of radwaste is a very significant challenge for which answers are still being sought. This starts with the mining and milling of the ore, with its naturally occurring 0.7% of uranium. Extracted from underground or opencast mines, uranium ore is processed to enrich it by increasing the proportion of uranium, to produce nuclear fuel. This is sometimes called the *front-end* of the nuclear fuel cycle: from the mining to the use of the uranium in the reactor. The *back-end* of the cycle involves the workings of the reactor and removal of the spent fuel and its treatment. Each end produces waste.

### Front-end radwaste

In underground mines especially, the control of dust is important. In uranium mines this is particularly so as long-term inhalation of uranium ore dust could have very harmful health effects. For this reason, dust is collected and processed along with the remainder of the mined material.

An additional challenge in uranium mines is the presence of radon gas. Radon is colourless, odourless and tasteless, and comes from the natural radioactive decay of uranium. It is radioactive and known to be carcinogenic, being said to be the second biggest cause of lung cancer after tobacco smoking. Large volumes of air are moved around the mines to reduce the concentration of radon and the mines have extensive ventilation systems with vertical shafts and fans built to ensure the dilution of the gas and to supply fresh air into the mines. The radon eventually disperses in the atmosphere.

After the ore has been removed from the ground, it is processed in a mill to extract the uranium. This process involves physical and chemical treatment of the ore. The uranium is leached from the ore using chemicals such as sulphuric acid. After a number of stages, most of the uranium is dissolved out of the ore and, with most of the uranium in a slurry form with some solids, it is washed to remove as much of the uranium as possible. Generally more than 95% of the uranium can be recovered from the ore in this way.

The remainder of the slurry, called tailings, is pumped to specially constructed cells with multiple clay and synthetic liners. This slurry is a mixture of solids from the ore, uranium which has not been recovered and the chemicals used in the leaching process. In consequence the uranium mill tailings are hazardous and this is why uranium processing mills are sited in areas where the potential impact on people is kept to a minimum. If the uranium mill is located close to the mine, the tailings may eventually be returned to the mine workings. In cases where this is not possible, they are covered with rock and soil and re-vegetated. The site is then monitored regularly to ensure that the covering is stable and that there is no environmental impact from the waste.

### Back-end radwaste

After the uranium has been extracted from the ore it is made into rods which provide the 'fuel' for the nuclear reactors. The operation of nuclear reactors provides a range of nuclear waste.

### Low-level Radioactive Waste

A large volume of waste with low levels of radioactivity is produced each year by the nuclear industry. These include contaminated items such as hand tools, paper, clothing and so on. Additionally the materials from which the reactors are built are also classed as low-level waste and have to be disposed of with care when nuclear power plants are decommissioned. It is not dangerous to handle this kind of waste but it is disposed of more carefully than normal waste. Largely it has its volume reduced by compaction or by incineration before going into special landfill sites. Low-level waste makes up 90% of the volume but only 1% of the radioactivity of all radwaste.

### Intermediate-level Radioactive Waste

Typically this contains higher levels of radioactivity than the low-level waste and it may require special shielding as a result. It includes resins and chemical sludges as well as contaminated materials from the decommissioning of reactors. It is treated in a number of ways. If the radiation is short-lived, the waste will be solidified in concrete or bitumen and then buried in shallow pits. If longer-lived radiation is present, it is typically stored deep underground in special facilities set up to secure and monitor the waste. This type of waste makes up 7% of the volume of radwaste in total, and accounts for 4% of the entire radioactivity.

### High-level Radioactive Waste

Much of the radioactivity of the radwaste comes from spent fuel rods from the nuclear plant. The fuel rods generally have a life of about 4 years, after which 3% of their uranium has been lost through fission. Then they are removed to basins of water or boric acid, sealed to prevent radioactive escape. Here the isotopes created by the fission, which generate short-term radioactivity, can decay. It is these spent fuel rods from a nuclear reactor which provide the biggest problem in dealing with nuclear waste, as they are the most radioactive of all nuclear wastes, giving off 99% of the total radioactivity when in that state. While only constituting 3% of the volume of all nuclear waste, high-level radwaste produces 95% of the radioactivity. Containing the highly-radioactive fission products and some elements with long-lived radioactivity, it generates a considerable heat and requires cooling and shielding to prevent radioactivity escaping during handling and transport. The length of time that high-level radioactive waste will have to be stored until it ceases to be hazardous ranges from 10,000 to 1,000,000 years.

The rods spend around 5 years in the cooling pond before the levels of heat and radioactivity reduces enough to allow them to be handled further. At that stage, still highly radioactive, there are two possibilities.

## 1. Storage

They can be moved to dry storage, where the spent fuel is encased in steel and concrete casks until its radioactivity decays to safe levels after decades or many thousands of years. Where these are then stored is another issue. Some countries have built up large stockpiles of spent fuel awaiting a decision as to long-term disposal. For example, the USA was said to have 50,000 tonnes of spent nuclear fuel from nuclear power plants in 2007. Permanent storage 450 metres underground at Yukka Mountain, Nevada has been suggested and the possibility of developing it as a nuclear waste repository is currently being assessed. As Yukka Mountain is in an extremely arid area of the USA, this minimises the risk of

*Yukka Mountain – possible site for a nuclear waste repository*

**Resource 16**

water seeping through the ground and corroding the casks. Even if corrosion did occur, the lack of water would reduce the possibility of the waste escaping. Additionally Yukka Mountain is in an area with a very low population density. The nearest city, Las Vegas, is 130 km south-east, and this further reduces the risks to people. Opponents point out that Yukka Mountain is on a fault line, but it is thought to be inactive.

### Deep storage or surface storage?

Many scientists believe that it would be prudent to store high-level nuclear waste **above ground** for 100 years or so. This allows the material to be more easily monitored to detect and manage any problems. The radioactive decay during this century of surface storage will reduce the level of radioactivity and the harmful effects that it may have on the container material. Also, over the century when the materials are being stored in the secure storage facilities, it is likely that scientists will develop materials that will contain the radioactivity for even longer. There is even a hope that science will find a use for the radioactive material which we presently classify as waste and that it will become a valuable resource in the future. However, this long-term storage combined with the required monitoring and the provision of security will be very expensive.

Other scientists favour the use of **deep burial** of the wastes. This involves the excavation of a large tunnel up to 1,000 m underground using equipment similar to that used to construct the Channel Tunnel. The tunnel would be constructed in a stable geological formation and would allow access to a number of vaults excavated from the rock. The nuclear waste deposited there would be permanently isolated from people and the environment.

As some radioactive materials have half-lives longer than one million years, even containers that deteriorate over very long periods of time would be of concern. In addition, it may take longer than one half-life before the radioactivity is low enough not to be lethal to living things. Whatever approach is taken, this will be a long-term concern.

## Resource 17   *Fuel transport*

Spent fuel flasks being transported by rail from Hinkley Point Power Station to Sellafield.

## Resource 18   *Reprocessing*

Spent fuel rod

Nitric Acid

High level waste turned into glass and stored

Uranium turned into new fuel pellets

Plutonium combined with uranium to produce mixed oxide fuel (MOX)

Returned to country of origin

The waste that such facilities are designed to store has to be stabilised in some way. One of these is vitrification. The advantage of vitrification is that it uses glass and the material produced is very resistant to water permeation. Sellafield in the UK treats high-level waste in this way. The waste is mixed with sugar and water is evaporated from it. This is then fed continuously into a furnace with glass, of a type similar to Pyrex, in beads of 1 or 2 mm in diameter. The resultant molten material, into which the radioactive substances are bonded, is poured into stainless steel containers where it solidifies (vitrifies) into a black glass-like substance. The stainless steel container is then sealed and washed. Each container is 1.3 m high with a 0.4 m diameter and weighs about 400 kg. After checking for external contamination, the steel cylinder is ready for storage. This process is expected to immobilise the radioactivity for a very long period, perhaps even thousands of years. The waste from a typical reactor for one year, once vitrified, would fill about twelve canisters. Vitrification plants in Europe produce about 2,500 canisters of vitrified waste each year.

Another technology which has recently become available is synroc (synthetic rock) developed by an Australian scientist. At present it is used for US military nuclear waste but it may come into use for non-military waste too. Some of the ingredients of the synthetic rock bind the nuclear materials and the solidified rock should be even more stable than that produced in the vitrification process. The radioactive wastes are incorporated in the crystalline structures of the naturally-stable minerals in a synthetic rock, therefore mimicking what happens in nature.

### 2. Reprocessing

This is the chemical operation which separates the useful fuel for recycling from the waste. One of the benefits is that this process reduces, although it does not entirely eliminate, the amount of waste requiring storage. There are only two commercial reprocessing plants in the world at present: Sellafield in the UK and Cogema in France. Japan is currently building a reprocessing plant at Rokkashomura, and China and India are also thought to be constructing nuclear reprocessing facilities.

In Sellafield, the Thorp reprocessing facility takes in waste from 34 nuclear power plants located in nine countries: UK, Japan, Germany, Switzerland, Spain, Sweden, Italy, Netherlands and Canada. Spent fuel rods are transported to the plant (**Resource 17**) and there the metallic outer casing is removed and the spent fuel dissolved in hot nitric acid (**Resource 18**). There are three products of such reprocessing: uranium (96%), plutonium (1%) and highly radioactive waste (3%).

The **uranium** can be turned into a powder and processed into fuel pellets for use in nuclear reactors.

The **plutonium** can be combined with uranium to produce a mixed oxide fuel (called Mox), which can be used in special Mox Nuclear Reactors. There are 6 g of Mox in each pellet, with the combined energy equivalent to one tonne of coal. British Nuclear Fuel (BNFL) claims that three such pellets would provide a family with all their energy needs for one year.

Plutonium is also the main material used in atomic weapons and there is a concern that reprocessed Mox material could easily have the plutonium removed from it by terrorists to manufacture an atomic bomb. Only about 9 kg of plutonium are required to construct an atomic bomb and, unlike uranium, in the form of plutonium it is not too radioactive to steal. As a consequence of those concerns, the police guards escorting Mox shipments from Sellafield are Europe's most heavily armed, equipped with rifles, gas masks and grenades. To guard against attack, naval cannon were mounted in the two ships carrying the first Mox shipment to Japan. In addition, the cargo hold was welded shut and the cranes on the ships used to load and unload the containers were removed before they set off on their voyage.

The 3% remaining **high-level waste** is turned into a powder and made into pellets by being mixed with glass. This is then stored for eventual return to the country of origin.

There are many advantages of reprocessing. BNFL claim that the reprocessing of one tonne of spent fuel saves about 100,000 barrels of oil, and helps to conserve the world's uranium supplies, which at current rates of use will run out in 175 years. 97% of the nuclear waste can be recycled through this natural method and, if it were not reprocessed, it would require more storage.

Critics point out that, while the reprocessing may reduce the volume that is required to be stored, it does not solve the challenges of nuclear waste storage. Some people point to other disadvantages of reprocessing. Environmentalists claim that reprocessing in Sellafield has resulted in increased cancer rates in the area. Ireland is concerned about a major increase in radioactivity in the Irish Sea. Even Norway has voiced concerns about radioactivity being carried from Sellafield to its coastline, by prevailing ocean currents. Opponents of reprocessing also point to the increased risk of terrorists obtaining plutonium for nuclear weapons, or of other countries getting hold of plutonium and increasing nuclear weapon proliferation.

## Past Papers

* While questions that have been set for a different specification should be used with great care, and the approach to assessment is very different in Global Issues, the following past paper questions (2007 and 2009) and their resources are still useful.

**Exercise**

### Figure 1

**Chernobyl disaster linked to higher rate of infant mortality in Britain**

The debate over the health effects of the Chernobyl nuclear disaster in Britain reopens today with research which suggests that infant deaths were higher in areas where rain fell as the plume of fallout passed overhead.

A study by the epidemiologist John Urquhart, to be presented at a conference at City Hall in London marking the 20th anniversary of the disaster, suggests that infant deaths may have risen by 11 per cent between 1986 and 1989 in those areas compared with 4 per cent in other areas …

Mr Urquhart … obtained infant death figures from 1983 to 1992 for 200 hospital districts across Britain. Areas across which cloud passed such as Liverpool, Bradford, Leicestershire, and Bristol, showed higher than average infant mortality which, he suggests, cannot entirely be explained by social factors …

Mr Urquhart argues that a plume of fallout from Chernobyl arrived near the Isle of Wight and passed over Bristol into south Wales. Another plume clipped the coast of Kent and then covered most of East Anglia and part of Essex. Another worked its way from east London to Hertfordshire, resurfacing in parts of Northamptonshire and Leicestershire. Parts of West Yorkshire and most of the West Midlands, Wales, Merseyside, Lancashire, and Cumbria were significantly affected.

Mr Urquhart, who gave evidence in the 1980s to the Government investigation led by Sir Douglas Black into evidence of a leukaemia cluster near Sellafield, Cumbria, said: "Previous research has established that there has been an increase in thyroid cancers in the young in the north of England for which Chernobyl is the probable cause. "This new study shows that the infant mortality trend, which was otherwise downwards, rose for a period of four years in England and Wales after Chernobyl. The results based on such a large population suggest that the effect of radioactive fallout could be … greater than previously suspected."

*'Chernobyl disaster linked to higher rate of infant mortality in Britain', 23 March 2006,*
*The Independent, © 2006 Independent Print Limited*

### Figure 2

**Expanding nuclear instead of green energy 'could save billions'**

Building a new generation of nuclear power stations would be a much cheaper way of meeting the UK's ambitious targets for cutting greenhouse gas emissions than persisting with an expansion of renewable energy, according to research published today.

The analysis, by the economics consultancy Oxera, calculates that a new nuclear programme would cost the taxpayer just over £4 bn whereas continuing to rely on green energy such as wind power would require £12 bn of public support.

The Government has set a target of reducing the UK's carbon emissions by 60% by 2050 and producing 20% of the country's electricity from renewable sources by 2020. However, Oxera calculates that by 2025, the UK will be running 40–60% short of its carbon-reduction targets … unless there is a much bigger shift away from fossil fuel electricity generation than currently envisaged.

Robin Smale, Oxera's managing consultant, said: "At the moment, the two options available are increasing the amount of nuclear-generated energy or increasing renewables at the taxpayer's expense – neither of which will be popular. From the point of view of the taxpayer, nuclear energy may be a strong contender given its costs relative to wind power."

*'Expanding nuclear instead of green energy 'could save billions' , 25 April 2005, The Independent, © 2005 Independent Print Limited*

**Figures 1 and 2 adapted from resources for CCEA January 2009**

1. *Question adapted from CCEA January 2009*

   What does **Figure 1** indicate about the limitations of our knowledge of the impacts of radiation pollution?    (5)

2. *Question from CCEA January 2007*

   Study **Figure 2** which is a newspaper article concerning the future of nuclear energy in the United Kingdom.

   (i) Using the resource to help you, describe the potential positive impacts of the development of nuclear-generated energy.    (7)

   (ii) Using the resource, evaluate the United Kingdom Government's policy of increasing energy generation through the use of a combination of nuclear energy and renewable power.    (5)

# THE NUCLEAR DEBATE

**Resource 19** *Dungeness nuclear power plant in Kent, England*

**Resource 20** *Torness nuclear power station, in East Lothian, Scotland*

## Local attitudes and issues related to nuclear energy

Most of the UK's nuclear power plants are ageing structures nearing the end of their lives as power stations. Most will have to be decommissioned by 2023. Some experts are concerned that this will leave the UK short of power generation capacity. In late 2009, the British government approved the building of ten new nuclear power stations in England and Wales. The Scottish National Party, currently in charge of the Scottish parliament, opposes any further development of nuclear power in Scotland – it currently has two nuclear plants operating. Northern Ireland has never had a nuclear power station. Most of those proposed are at sites where nuclear power plants already exist or existed in the past (**Resource 21**). Only one of the proposed plants was rejected by the government. It was to have been in Kent, at Dungeness, and it was deemed an unsuitable site. While Dungeness has an existing plant (**Resource 19**), the government rejected the proposal because of the prospective damage to the delicate coastal ecosystem (Dungeness is a cuspate foreland rather like Magilligan in Northern Ireland) and dangers related to coastal flooding and erosion. Two wholly new sites are under consideration: Braystones and Kirksanton, both in Cumbria.

The UK government approval does not mean that these plants will necessarily be built – they face a planning commission first – but it is a sign that the nuclear route is one which the British government has embraced.

It has been pointed out that most people living close to nuclear power plants are enthusiastic about them and that the new plants will generate 9,000 jobs. The government plan is to fast-track the nuclear power plants through the planning process.

This decision is controversial. Many environmentalists claim that nuclear is an expensive option, which produces problems of toxic waste. Those in favour of the proposal point to the savings in carbon production over conventional power generation using coal, oil or gas. The Irish Government are concerned about the proposals too, as seven of the proposed new plants are on the Irish Sea coastline of England and Wales, directly opposite large Irish population centres. They have been seeking the closure of the Sellafield nuclear processing facility for many years, and yet it is the proposed site for one of the proposed new reactors. The Fine Gael representative for county Louth, Fergus O'Dowd argues: "People are concerned over here about the possibility of an accident or an act of terrorism. If the prevailing wind was blowing in our direction, we'd get the hit."

**Proposed sites for new nuclear power stations in England and Wales**  **Resource 21**

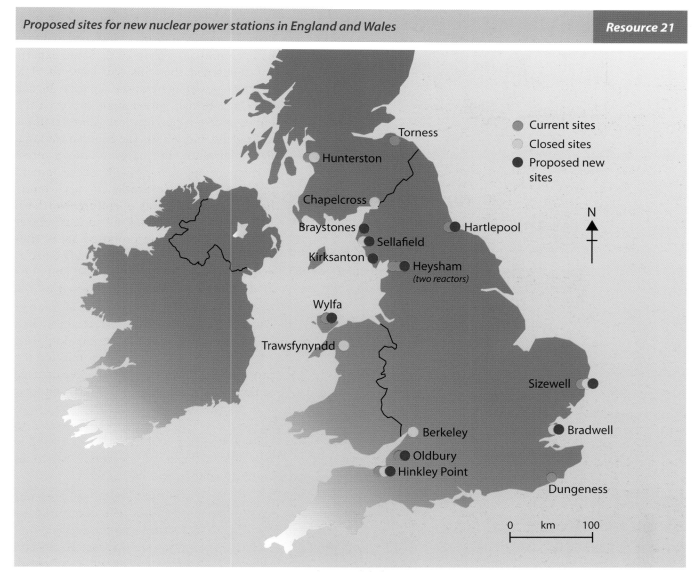

Source: Data from Department of Energy and Climate Change (DECC), www.decc.gov.uk

**Resource 22**    *The Olkiluoto unit 3 reactor, Finland, 2009*

## Issues concerning nuclear energy development

- Cost: There are few recent examples of the building of nuclear power plants but one being built currently in Finland, which is Europe's first new plant in the last 10 years, is expected to cost £2.25 billion (**Resource 22).** This is much more expensive that building coal or gas powered plants, which come in at a mere £900 million each. However, nuclear plants have the advantage that, once built, they are much cheaper to run than other types of power plants.

- Greenhouse gases: Lower levels of greenhouse gas emissions from nuclear plants may make this type of power generation more and more attractive, with climate change having an increased impact.

- Decommissioning costs: The cost of decommissioning old plants and of waste storage should be taken into account when working out how much a nuclear power plant actually costs.

The proposals to develop nuclear energy in the UK have attracted much debate:

"The threat of climate change means we need to make a transition from a system that relies heavily on high-carbon fossil fuels, to a radically different system that includes nuclear, renewable and clean coal power."

*Ed Miliband, Labour Energy and Climate Change Secretary*

"You can't justify building more nuclear power stations when there is no solution to radioactive waste and when international regulators are saying there are huge uncertainties surrounding the basic safety of new reactor designs."

*Ben Aycliffe, Greenpeace*

"These planning statements will help reassure companies that the government has a clear strategy for delivering new nuclear power, clean coal and renewable energy plants, and that this will be reflected in planning decisions."

*Confederation of British Industry*

"A new generation of nuclear power stations will be a colossal mistake regardless of where they are built. New plants in the UK have never been built without massive cost to the taxpayer and a lethal legacy of toxic waste."

*Simon Hughes, Liberal Democrat Energy and Climate Change spokesperson*

**Exercise**

1. *Question from CCEA January 2010*

   With reference to the British Isles and other places for illustration, evaluate the extent of the actual and potential problems associated with nuclear energy generation.    (20)

2. *Question from CCEA Specimen Paper 2010*

   "We should not rely on nuclear energy because of the inevitable pollution risks, both actual and potential."

   Evaluate the evidence that can be presented in support of this statement.    (20)

2. *Question from CCEA Summer 2010*

   "Nuclear energy provides the solution to pollution in the British Isles and other places."

   Justify the extent to which you agree with this statement.    (20)

# PRIMARY INVESTIGATION

You could look at local attitudes to the proposal described on pages 34–35, or you could examine attitudes to nuclear energy more generally. There are a number of studies suggested here which you can explore for ideas as to what sorts of questions would be interesting, or you may well come up with some of your own and approach your investigation from a different angle. A recent Australian study, for example, conducted by a newspaper, *The Australian*, produced the results summarised in **Resource 23**.

| **Resource 23** | *Summary of results from a survey by* The Australian *newspaper (April 2007)* |
| --- | --- |

## Support for construction of nuclear power plants

\* Note: Totals may not add to 100 due to rounding.

| | |
| --- | --- |
| Strongly support the construction of nuclear power plants | 16% |
| Support the construction of nuclear power plants | 21% |
| **Total in favour** | **37%** |
| Strongly opposed to the construction of nuclear power | 31% |
| Opposed to the construction of nuclear power | 15% |
| **Total opposed** | **46%** |
| Don't know | 18% |

## Greatest opposition to nuclear power by various groups in Australia

| | |
| --- | --- |
| Women | 55% |
| Young | 49% |
| Middle aged | 49% |
| Parents | 50% |
| Middle income households | 49% |
| Residents of Tasmania | 57% |
| Residents of Western Australia | 55% |
| Residents of Victoria | 51% |

## Greatest support for nuclear power by various groups in Australia

| | |
| --- | --- |
| Men | 47% |
| Older age groups | 43% |
| Adults without children | 40% |
| Residents of South Australia | 47% |
| Residents of New South Wales | 41% |

Full results, including comparisons with earlier surveys, are available at The Australia Institute website: https://www.tai.org.au/documents/downloads/WP99.pdf

Source: 'Attitudes to Nuclear Power. Are they Shifting?', The Australia Institute, Research Paper No 43, May 2007

Studies in the UK also show that certain groups are more or less likely to support nuclear power. Here too the age of the person asked seemed to have an effect on the viewpoint. In a number of surveys (eg *Populus: the daily politics: how green are we?* ICM Research for BBC Newsnight, 2005), it was found that older people tend to be more in favour of nuclear energy than young people. The studies looking at gender differences also show that, for men, nuclear power is much preferred over wind power (33% compared to women's 11%). An individual's social class and income was also seen to have an impact on their attitudes. People earning more than £30,000 per year, and those in social classes A and B, were more in favour of nuclear power development than those on lower incomes and from social classes D and E. There also seems to be some evidence that more informed people are more accepting of nuclear energy development. Even political viewpoint may have an impact on the attitudes taken. For example, the Populus poll of 2005 suggested that 37% of individuals who support the Conservative party would support the development of new nuclear power stations, while the proportion of Labour and Liberal Democrat supporters were only 12% and 14% respectively.

Your primary research will shed a lot of light on the attitudes to nuclear power of your sample – enjoy!

You can view the results of the above polls at:

Minnesota Opinion Research Inc (MORI):

http://populuslimited.com/uploads/download_pdf-060706-The-Daily-Politics-How-Green-are-We.pdf

ICM Research:

http://www.icmresearch.co.uk/pdfs/2006_july_gmtv_energy_poll.pdf#search=%22GMTV%22

*Exercise*

1. *Question from CCEA January 2010*

   With reference to your primary data collection relating to nuclear energy, describe one data collection technique used and comment briefly on the effectiveness of this technique.    (4)

2. *Question from CCEA Summer 2010*

   With reference to your primary data collection relating to nuclear energy, state the aim(s) of your investigation and explain what the results show.    (6)

3. *Question from CCEA Specimen Paper 2010*

   With reference to your primary data collection, state your aim(s) and explain how the results helped your understanding of nuclear energy.    (6)

## Additional References

### Websites

'Nuclear power and nuclear weapons', Nuclear Energy Information Service – www.neis.org/literature/Brochures/weapcon.htm

'Timeline: nuclear accidents', BBC News – http://news.bbc.co.uk/1/hi/sci/tech/5165736.stm

'Go-ahead for 10 nuclear power stations', BBC News – http://news.bbc.co.uk/1/hi/uk_politics/8349715.stm

'Dounreay 50th anniversary marked', BBC News – http://news.bbc.co.uk/1/hi/scotland/highlands_and_islands/8346190.stm

'Electricity calculator', BBC News – http://news.bbc.co.uk/1/shared/spl/hi/uk/06/electricity_calc/html/1.stm

'Q&A: The costs of nuclear power', BBC News – http://news.bbc.co.uk/1/hi/business/7180539.stm

'Ten UK nuclear power stations by 2010', Telegraph – www.telegraph.co.uk/earth/earthnews/3321124/Ten-UK-nuclear-power-stations-by-2020.html#form

Nuclear Power: a dangerous waste of time (Greenpeace) – www.greenpeace.org/raw/content/usa/press-center/reports4/nuclear-power-a-dangerous-was.pdf

'Seven of Britain's new nuclear plants will be on Irish Sea Coast', Belfast Telegraph – www.belfasttelegraph.co.uk/news/local-national/seven-of-britainrsquos-new-nuclear-plants-will-be-on-irish-sea-coast-14557126.html

Impact of Chernobyl on UK farming, Food Standards Agency – www.food.gov.uk/science/surveillance/radiosurv/chernobyl/

No2 Nuclear Power [a campaigning group opposed to nuclear power] – www.no2nuclearpower.org.uk/

# ISSUES IN TOURISM

# THE CHANGING NATURE AND CHARACTERISTICS OF TOURISM

Tourism refers to all temporary visits to a new destination that include at least one overnight stay. The new destination can be local, regional or international. International tourists are referred to as **arrivals** or **incoming tourists** in their destination country and as **outbound tourists** from their home country. There are many types of tourism including recreation, visiting friends and relatives (VFR), religious pilgrimages, health, sport and business. Recreation is the main underlying reason for increases in tourism, accounting for over 50% of international tourism (**Resource 24**). Air and road transport are the main forms of transport used (**Resource 25**).

Tourism has immense economic impacts and international tourism is one of the world's largest export industries. International tourism is regarded as an export because it brings foreign money into the receiving country. The overall export income generated by international tourism in 2008 was US$944 billion. Globally, tourism exports account for 30% of the world's exports of commercial services, ranking fourth after fuels, chemicals and motor vehicles. The tourist industry creates new employment opportunities in the service sector, construction work, food processing, transport and many others. If tourism were a country, it would have the second largest economy, surpassed only by the US. In many LEDCs, tourism is one of the main income sources and the number one export category, creating much needed employment and opportunities for development (**Resource 26**).

## Growth of international tourism

Tourism, and international tourism in particular, has experienced three major changes since the 1960s.

1. An increase in the number of tourists.
2. An increase in the distance travelled by tourists.
3. An increase in the range and diversity of holiday types – seaside, skiing, ecotourism.

| Resource 24 | International tourism by purpose of visit |

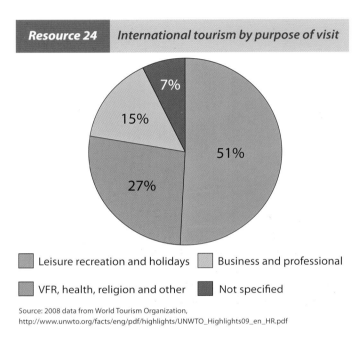

- Leisure recreation and holidays
- Business and professional
- VFR, health, religion and other
- Not specified

Source: 2008 data from World Tourism Organization,
http://www.unwto.org/facts/eng/pdf/highlights/UNWTO_Highlights09_en_HR.pdf

| Resource 25 | International tourism by means of transport |

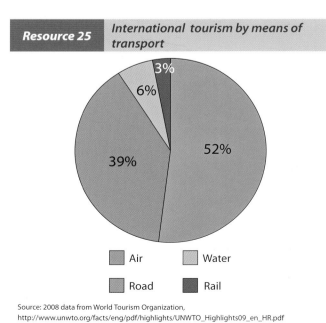

- Air
- Water
- Road
- Rail

Source: 2008 data from World Tourism Organization,
http://www.unwto.org/facts/eng/pdf/highlights/UNWTO_Highlights09_en_HR.pdf

**World exports of merchandise and commercial services (balance of payments, goods and services credit)**   *Resource 26*

|  | US$ billion | Share (%) | Share (%) |
|---|---|---|---|
| **Total** | **9089** | **100** | |
| **Merchandise exports** | **7294** | **80** | |
| Agricultural products | 674 | 7 | |
| Mining products | 960 | 11 | |
| Manufactures | 5437 | 60 | |
| Other | 223 | 2 | |
| **Commercial services** | **1795** | **20** | **100** |
| Transportation | 405 | 4 | 23 |
| Travel | 525 | 6 | 29 |
| Other | 865 | 10 | 48 |

Source: World Trade Organization, World Tourism Organization, http://www.unwto.org/facts/eng/economy.htm

The increase in tourist numbers and the distances travelled are closely related to the growth in international tourism. Tourism started in the nineteenth century and from then until the mid twentieth century remained the privilege of the wealthy. The phenomenal growth in tourist numbers since then is the result of tourism becoming more accessible to a greater number of people. This is due to a number of factors including increased prosperity and improved working conditions. Workers are now paid better wages and this has led to increased disposable incomes. Government legislation guarantees workers paid holiday time off work and this has enabled most workers to have at least one annual break away from home. Higher income groups are able to afford several holidays away from home each year. Developments in transport have improved accessibility and in recent time the 'no frills' or budget airlines have made international tourism relatively cheap.

**Growth in international tourism 1950–2008 (projected for 2020)**   *Resource 27*

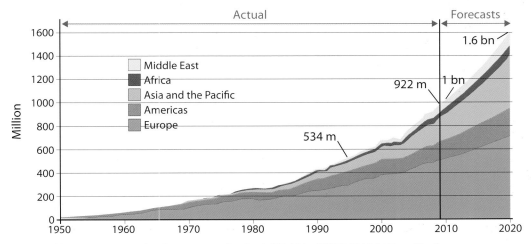

Source: World Tourism Organization, http://www.unwto.org/facts/eng/pdf/highlights/UNWTO_Highlights09_en_HR.pdf

*Exercise*

Study **Resource 27** and describe the patterns and trends in international tourism.

The introduction of the 'package holiday' had a very significant impact on international tourism. Package holidays remove many of the obstacles to international tourism, such as language barriers. They provide an all in deal for tourists whereby a travel company arranges all aspects of the holiday from flights, accommodation, transport to and from the holiday airport, and offer tours and activities to the tourist. The birth of the package holiday can be traced back to Thomas Cook when he organised what is considered to be the first package holiday from Leicester to Loughborough in 1863. Several years later he organised the first international package deal to Europe. Currently, the Thomas Cook organisation is one of the world's leading travel agencies employing over 30,000 people, has over 22 million customers, a fleet of 93 aircraft and operates in 21 countries. Package holidays also led to the development of mass tourism, where a large number of tourists are concentrated in a few well developed holiday resorts. Now tourists can arrange their own tailor made holiday on the Internet, often cheaper than using the services of a travel agent.

## Global Patterns of Tourism

In 2008 there were 922 million tourist arrivals and this figure is predicted to continue to grow, reaching 1.6 billion by 2020. More than half of the 2008 arrivals (489 million) went to a European destination. A further 10% went to North America. This emphasises the point that tourism is still dominated by MEDCs due to the greater levels of wealth and development than in LEDCs. However, this pattern is changing and, increasingly, the LEDCs are developing their tourism potential. Since the 1990s newly emerging tourist destinations in Africa, Asia/Pacific and the Middle East have all experienced rapid growth rates in the number of tourist arrivals (**Resource 27**). In fact tourism is regarded as a vital element in the Millennium Development Goals' targets to alleviate poverty. In addition, China and India are becoming major economic powers and as disposable income rises so do the number of tourists. As China becomes more open to the outside world it will receive even more visitors from Europe and America. Improvements in transport have also facilitated the growth of long haul flights and these are projected to double by 2020.

Tourism is driven by economic growth with the strongest increases occurring in times of economic success and a slowing down in times of economic downturn. In recent times the peak growth year was 2006/7 when a 6% increase in numbers was recorded. In 2008 the number of

| Resource 28 | International tourist arrivals by region (millions) | | |
| --- | --- | --- | --- |
| | **1995** | **2010** | **2020** |
| **Total** | **565** | **1006** | **1561** |
| Africa | 20 | 47 | 77 |
| Americas | 109 | 190 | 282 |
| East Asia/Pacific | 81 | 195 | 397 |
| Europe | 338 | 527 | 717 |
| Middle East | 12 | 36 | 69 |
| South Asia | 4 | 11 | 19 |

*Figures in brackets indicate numbers of tourist arrivals in millions.

Source: Data for both Resources from World Tourism Organization, http://www.unwto.org

| Resource 29 | The top ten tourism destinations 1995, 2005 and 2007 | | |
| --- | --- | --- | --- |
| **Rank** | **1995** | **2005** | **2007** |
| 1 | France (67) | France (76) | France (82) |
| 2 | USA (49) | Spain (56) | USA (57) |
| 3 | Spain (43) | USA (49) | Spain (59) |
| 4 | Italy (34) | China (47) | China (55) |
| 5 | UK (26) | Italy (36) | Italy (44) |
| 6 | China (24) | UK (30) | UK (31) |
| 7 | Poland (20) | Mexico (22) | Ukraine (23) |
| 8 | Mexico (19) | Germany (21) | Turkey (22) |
| 9 | Canada (18) | Turkey (20) | Germany (24) |
| 10 | Czech Republic (17) | Austria (19) | Mexico (22) |

international tourist arrivals reached 922 million representing a 2% growth from the previous year. This slower rate of growth reflects the global economic problems which started in 2008. An interesting development has been the growth of tourism in Turkey and Eastern Europe – partly explained by more favourable exchange rates in Turkey and the relatively lower prices in Eastern Europe.

---

**Exercise**

Study the information in **Resources 28 and 29**:

(a) Describe the patterns shown.

(b) Suggest possible reasons for these patterns.

---

## Range of holiday types

Along side the developments in transport and increased prosperity there has been an increase in the range of holidays provided. For a long time tourism and holidays were mostly confined to the summer season. Now there is a demand for holidays throughout the year. In addition to the traditional seaside summer holidays there are now winter holidays skiing or snowboarding and the warmer Mediterranean resorts are also popular during the 'off-peak' season for some of the retired population from Northern Europe. With greater amounts of information available on the Internet and the media other tourist opportunities are developing. These include:

- Cultural and historical breaks – Rome and Athens, stately homes in Britain
- Theme parks – Euro Disney
- Adventure tourism – Himalayas, Antarctica
- Ecotourism (environmentally friendly or green tourism) – Costa Rica

---

*There is a vast range of holiday types available today*     **Resource 30**

The Pantheon, Rome (cultural and historical tourism)

Euro Disney (theme parks)

Mountaineering in France (adventure tourism)

Waddesdon Manor, Buckinghamshire (cultural and historical tourism)

Biking in South America (adventure tourism)

## Tourism Models

Tourism is a dynamic industry. Tourist destinations and tourists' demands change and evolve over time. A number of models have been devised to explain these changes. Some of the models examine the changing demands of the tourist while others examine the evolution of the tourist resort.

| Resource 31 | *The Pleasure Periphery* |
| --- | --- |

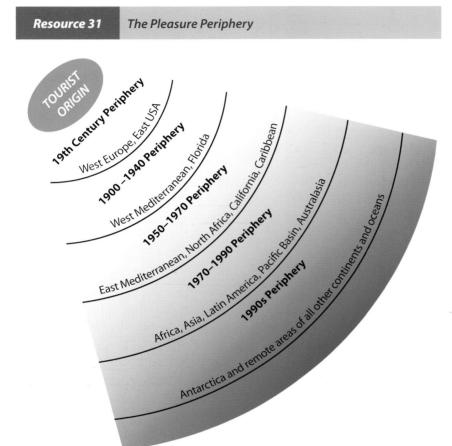

### 1. Pleasure Periphery

This model focuses on the behavioural demands of the tourist over time. With increased prosperity and improvements in transport technology long distance travel has been made easier. Mass media and advertising play a large role in promoting new and more exotic tourist destinations. Expectations are increased and tourism is envisaged as a 'fashion industry' where tourists want to spend their holidays in the new and more fashionable resorts. The boundaries of tourism are seen as a tidal wave spreading outwards from the tourists' home area. The example of the changing pattern of British tourism illustrates this concept (**Resource 32**).

Other likely developments include space tourism and underwater hotels – one of which is already in existence in Dubai.

| Resource 32 | *Changing pattern of British tourism* |
| --- | --- |

### Pleasure Periphery Changes in Britain

- In the nineteenth century wealthy British tourists spent their holidays at British seaside resorts.
- In the 1950s and 60s package holidays to specially developed holiday camps such as Butlins became popular.
- From the 1960s cheaper air travel and package holidays to the Spanish seaside resorts became popular.
- In the 1980s and 90s Florida and the Caribbean became more fashionable.
- More recently trips to Asia and Australia are growing in demand.
- In the future cruises to Antarctica and other remote areas may become popular.

## 2. Product Cycle

This model examines the evolution of a tourist resort over time. All tourist resorts develop around some form of attraction – coastal, mountains or scenery. The product cycle model views tourism as an exploitive industry, such as mining of a finite resource, whereby the attractions of the tourist resort are exploited to the full. This situation may result in over development and the region begins to lose its pulling power for tourists and may go into decline. The tourist then seeks new attractions elsewhere. This model can be used to show evolution of a single tourist resort in time or it can locate different resorts on the model at one specific time period (**Resources 33a and 33b**).

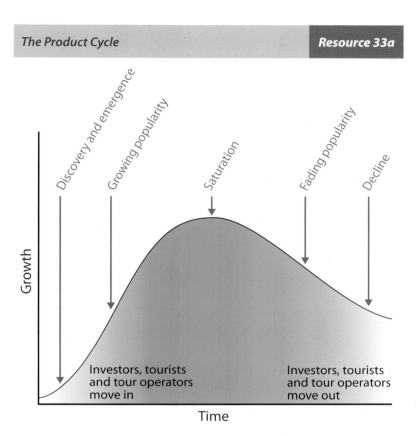

**The Product Cycle** — *Resource 33a*

Discovery and emergence — Growing popularity — Saturation — Fading popularity — Decline

Growth / Time

Investors, tourists and tour operators move in

Investors, tourists and tour operators move out

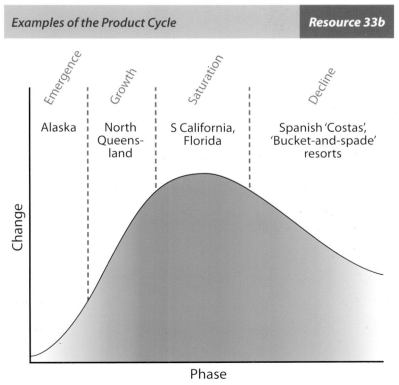

**Examples of the Product Cycle** — *Resource 33b*

Emergence — Growth — Saturation — Decline

Alaska | North Queensland | S California, Florida | Spanish 'Costas', 'Bucket-and-spade' resorts

Change / Phase

**Resource 34   The Butler Model**

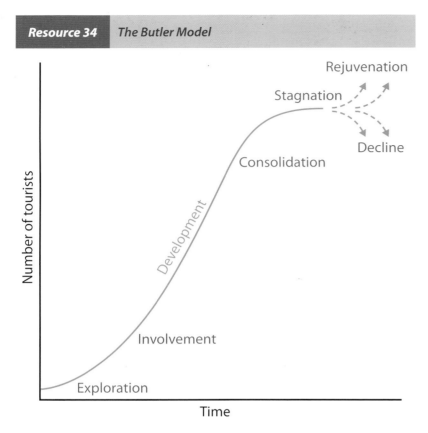

## 3. Butler Model

Product Cycle is in a sense a predictive model which sees all tourist resorts having a finite life span. However, it has been shown that not all tourist resorts follow this inevitable path towards decline. Tourism management policies can prolong or revitalise the fortunes of a tourist destination. The Butler Model (**Resource 34**) is a refinement of the Product Cycle by incorporating the possibility of human intervention through management policies.

There are six stages in this process, which are shown below:

### (i) Exploration

At the beginning of a resort's life cycle there are only a few tourists and minimum impact.

### (ii) Involvement

In time the resort grows in popularity and the number of tourists increases. New developments including hotels, recreational facilities and general infrastructure are added. New employment opportunities for local people arise although most of these are seasonal.

### (iii) Development

Tourist numbers increase leading to mass tourism and the development of package holidays. Much of the tourist trade and the wealth it generates are controlled and managed by international organisations to the detriment of the local economy.

### (iv) Consolidation

Tourism is now a major industry in the region. The control of the industry lies with the international organisations. The local area does benefit from the developments such as infrastructure and seasonal employment but decisions over the allocation of resources often favour tourism over local needs (see case study of Mallorca, pages 56–61).

### (v) Stagnation

The resort then becomes very developed and eventually it suffers from over development or saturation.

### (vi) Decline/rejuvenation

Saturation is followed by stagnation and decline with loss of popularity for tourists and the international organisations. It is possible for a resort to recover from decline through a comprehensive management policy, a process known as **rejuvenation.**

# THE CONSEQUENCES OF TOURISM CHANGE

Tourism inevitably has impacts on a region and those impacts can be positive or negative. As mentioned earlier, tourism is a vital source of export revenue for many countries and it provides employment for large numbers of people. The money generated from tourism can help fund the development of infrastructure, education and health projects. However, it has been shown that tourism, and in particular mass tourism, can have adverse effects on a region (see Butler Model, page 48). Mass tourism in the Mediterranean resorts from the 1960s onwards paid little attention to the long-term impacts on these regions. Short-term economic gain took precedence over potential environmental issues. In recent times most tourist areas have adopted a more sustainable approach to tourism development including some form of management.

A number of issues/conflicts have arisen in many resorts as a consequence of tourism development.

## Pollution

Anything that detracts from or causes actual harm to a tourist attraction is a major concern for tourist resorts. Pollution, in the form of damaged landscapes or habitats, increased noise levels, litter and waste disposal issues, is one of the main negative impacts of tourism. Increased numbers of tourists visiting a resort put seasonal pressure on the resources of that area. In the case of rural tourism to country parks, the attraction is often the quiet, peaceful and scenic landscape. An influx of tourists will bring welcome revenue but the provision of amenities such as car parks, caravan sites and shops can damage the scenic attraction of the area, cause footpath erosion and threaten wildlife habitats. In addition, some areas attract large numbers of tourists (**honeypot sites**) and these can become overcrowded. In time, the area risks changes that could damage the tourist potential. In the UK a number of management strategies have been devised to protect/manage the attractions of these rural areas. These strategies include the creation of National Parks, AONBs and ASSIs. More details on these strategies are available from *AS Geography For CCEA* (Colourpoint, 2008), pages 126–134.

Along the Mediterranean coasts the rapid influx of tourists in the summer season puts extra demands on the waste disposal capacity of that area. There were many reported claims of raw sewage in the sea and in 1989 the Spanish tourist resort of Salou had an outbreak of typhoid. Since then a number of improvements have been introduced and more careful management of waste disposal has brought beneficial effects. The Mediterranean region also experienced large-scale building of high-rise apartments and hotel blocks resulting in overcrowded beaches and spoilt scenery. Further environmental damage was caused

*High-rise buildings, Benidorm, Spain*  **Resource 35**

by the construction of artificial beaches, where sand was excavated from the sea bed and transported to another area in order to extend beach facilities there. Such activities alter the natural balance between erosion and deposition as well as impacting on the biodiversity of the area. Furthermore, budget airlines and low cost package holidays facilitated ever increasing numbers to visit the region. The main tourist areas also developed shops, restaurants, nightclubs, bars and other recreational activities for the growing number of tourists. These developments inevitably caused noise pollution. A number of these resorts have undertaken policies including restricting the height and density of buildings, upgrading waste disposal systems and introducing a tourist tax to be spent on more sustainable tourist developments.

Fragile landscapes are particularly vulnerable to environmental pollution from tourist developments. There are 109 countries with coral reefs and in 90 of these, reefs are being damaged by cruise ship anchors, sewage, tourists breaking off chunks of coral and commercial harvesting of coral for sale to tourists. Cruise ships in the Caribbean are estimated to produce more than 70,000 tons of waste each year.

Tourism relies on efficient transport infrastructure, including airports and roads, and these have major potential for environmental pollution. High altitude skiing areas require cable cars, ski lifts and possibly funicular railways, resulting in extensive forest clearance. The laying of ski runs can lead to erosion and loss of biodiversity. In Switzerland, where skiing is a major industry, there are also 23 mountain heliports, all above 1,100 m and handling 15,000 passengers annually. In addition, the skiing industry generates a large volume of waste. About 65% of this waste is non-biodegradable plastic and is disposed of in incinerators or is taken to landfills. Switzerland also has well developed mountaineering and hill walking tourist activities, which threaten the environment through trampling, footpath erosion and damage to wildlife habitats.

Since the late 1980s Switzerland has pursued a more sustainable form of tourist development. The Swiss Agency for the Environment, Forests and Landscape (SAEFL) has worked in collaboration with government departments to reduce the negative effects of existing tourist developments and all new developments are subject to an environmental risk assessment before planning permission is granted. Additional information is available from 'The Growth of Tourism in Switzerland', *Geofile* Online, January 2003 (Nelson Thornes, 2003).

| Resource 36 | Dead coral in a reef in the Philippines |
|---|---|

| Resource 37 | Annual waste generated from skiing in Switzerland |
|---|---|

| Skiing equipment | 43,000 tonnes |
|---|---|
| Sports footwear | 2,800 tonnes |
| Sports clothing | 4,000 tonnes |

Source: Data from 'The Growth of Tourism in Switzerland', *Geofile* Online, January 2003 (Nelson Thornes, 2003)

## Carrying Capacity

The term carrying capacity is often used in Geography to imply an upper limit or threshold population that can be supported by an area. In relation to tourism, the carrying capacity of a resort refers to the maximum number of tourists that can be comfortably supported in that resort. An increase in tourist numbers would adversely affect the tourist potential of the area and lead to a decline in numbers (**Resource 38**).

**A model of carrying capacity**                                    **Resource 38**

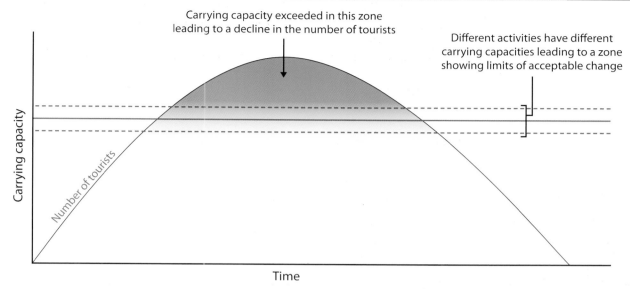

Source: Adapted from a diagram by Kim Adams published in 'Recreation, Tourism and Carrying Capacity: A Case Study of the Impacts of Visitors in a Rural/Wilderness area: Machu Picchu, Peru', *Geofile Online*, January 2008 (Nelson Thornes, 2008)

Essentially there are two components involved in assessing the carrying capacity of a tourist resort:

1. The maximum number of people that can be supported without causing adverse environmental impacts in the region, such as footpath erosion or vegetation trampling. This is sometimes referred to as the **physical carrying capacity.**

2. The maximum number of people that can be supported without causing a decline in visitor enjoyment of an attraction, sometimes referred to as the **quality of visitor experience**.

Physical carrying capacity is relatively easy to measure because the environmental outcomes (footpath erosion, damaged habitats) are obvious. However, setting a numerical limit on the numbers of people that can be supported without damaging the quality of visitor experience is much more subjective and will vary between types of tourist activity and the personality traits of the tourists themselves. Some tourist activities, such as hill walking, will typically have a lower carrying capacity than beach holidays. However, these are not absolute facts and there are many examples of large groups involved in hill walking. Furthermore, there are added difficulties or conflicts between different types of tourist activities in the same region. In the Peak District National Park the National Park Authorities introduced a zoning plan whereby conflicting users of the Park were restricted to specific areas. More detail on this strategy is available from *AS Geography For CCEA* (Colourpoint, 2008), pages 126–134.

Carrying Capacity also refers to the supply/demand balance of amenities in an area. This might include the provision of car parks, hotels and general infrastructure. Some of the issues relating to problems in the Mediterranean resorts dealt with in the pollution section are also closely related to carrying capacity.

**Hill walking in the Peak District**                               **Resource 39**

| Resource 40 | Management options in response to carrying capacity being exceeded |
| --- | --- |

| Reduce pressure by: | Increase capacity by: |
| --- | --- |
| • Restricting access in certain areas.<br>• Limiting access by charging entry fees, restricting parking, denying access to coaches.<br>• Using quotas to control the number of tourists visiting fragile sites.<br>• Developing new sites to disperse tourists from congested areas.<br>• Limiting numbers of second homes in tourist resorts. | • Controlling the distribution of people by concentrating amenities close to car parks and/or dispersing people to new attractions.<br>• Increasing resilience of the ecosystem, by planting resistant vegetation.<br>• Improving access by building new roads and bypasses.<br>• Timed ticket entry to reduce over crowding at specific times.<br>• Zoning of activities so that potential conflicting activities are kept apart.<br>• Influencing the type of activities by providing/ not providing facilities for specific activities. |

The latest approach to assessing the effects of increased numbers on the quality of visitor experience is known as Limits of Acceptable Change (LAC). This approach accepts that all tourism has impacts on a region and looks for ways to keep these impacts under control. In Arches National Park (Utah) a number of surveys were carried out to determine the number of visitors deemed acceptable in selected honeypot sites. Tourists were shown computer generated photographs of the sites occupied by different numbers of people ranging from 2 to over 100 and asked to state which numbers they considered acceptable and unacceptable. The tourists rated the impact of the numbers of people at any one time (PAOT) on a scale of -4 to +4. A positive value meant the resort had not been adversely affected by the numbers of people. A negative value meant the resort had been adversely affected. A value of zero indicates the maximum number that can be tolerated in the resort without damaging the quality of visitor experience (Limit of Acceptable Change). The results of the sample were averaged and drawn in **Resource 41**.

Essentially, carrying capacity is a framework within which those in charge of tourism can monitor developments in a region and formulate management policies if necessary. In some cases conservation orders, which are legally binding, are placed on an area to protect it from excessive and damaging use. These can be at local level such as SSIs or at regional level such as National Parks. There are also conservation policies at a European level, Special Areas of Conservation (SACs), which deal with wild life habitats and at international level, World Heritage Sites (sites that have global importance). Once carrying capacity has been reached tourist management policies can be employed to increase the carrying capacity or at least correct the damage (see case study of Mallorca, pages 56–61). However, in some cases this may not be possible and the resort will go into decline.

| Resource 41 | Acceptability ratings for numbers of people at any one time (PAOT) in Arches National Park, Utah (USA) |
| --- | --- |

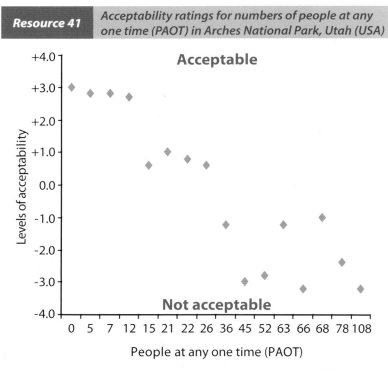

Source: Adapted from a graph published in 'Congestion, Crowding and Visitor Management in UK Country Parks', *Geofile Online*, April 2002 (Nelson Thornes, 2002)

Resource 42

## Venice slaps tax on its tourist tide

An estimated 14 million tourists visit Venice and its canals each year. The city authorities have now decided to impose a tax on tour buses. The tax, expected to raise £6 million pounds annually, makes this unique canal city the latest in a series of popular destinations attempting to introduce sustainable tourism. The aim of this tax is to control tourist numbers and provide funds for remedial work to infrastructure and environment, This has its opponents, notably tour operators and local hoteliers. Under this scheme a tax of £90 per day will be imposed on all coaches crossing the motorway that links this island city to the mainland. A tax is also levied on coaches travelling by ferry. If successful the tax could be extended to tourists arriving by train or cruise ship.

Venice's mayor claims the tax is the only way for the city, which has only 70,000 inhabitants, to deal with serious overcrowding by tourists and pressure on basic services. However, hoteliers affected by the global slow down in tourism, following the September 11th attacks on America, are strongly opposed to the scheme and plan to mount a legal challenge backed by associations representing small companies and coach operators. They claim the tax is illegal because it contravenes an ancient right to free movement in Venice. They also claim the authorities will use the money for projects other than those aimed at conservation of Venice's fragile environment.

© *The Sunday Times - March 2002* / nisyndication.com

Resource 43

More than 40% of the 58,000 tonnes of rubbish picked up each year is generated by tourists.

Pigeons fed by tourists damage the roofs of the historic buildings with their droppings.

Tourist impacts on Venice

The wash created by boats erodes the sides of the canals and the walls of buildings.

Sheer volume of visitors causes wear and tear on ancient monuments.

Resources 42 and 43 adapted from resources for CCEA January 2005

Exercise

1. Study **Resource 41** which shows the results of a questionnaire about carrying capacity of a National Park in Utah.

   (a) Comment on the patterns shown.

   (b) What factors would the researchers have needed to consider before carrying out the survey?

2. *Question from CCEA January 2005*

   Study **Resource 42** relating to tourism in Venice, Italy.

   Use the resources **to help you** discuss the need for a policy of sustainable tourism management in Venice.  (10)

## Competition for Resources

A tourist region requires investment in infrastructure (roads, airports) and amenities (hotels, entertainment). Such developments require vast amounts of money as well as land and water supplies. These things are often not in abundant supply and in such situations conflicts of interest can occur between the needs of the local community and the needs of the tourist industry. Tourism offers the potential of huge economic rewards and, as already stated, in some countries is a major export earner. Tourism offers the promise of foreign investment and, in many cases, when it comes to allocating scarce resources the needs of local people are sacrificed in the interests of the tourist industry. This competition for resources occurs worldwide but some of the most serious issues have been witnessed in the LEDCs or at least among poorer communities.

**Resource 44** — *Palm Springs golf course, California, with the desert in the background*

One of the significant tourist developments in the last 25 years has been golf tourism. The economic boom of the 1980s led to a worldwide growth in the number of golf courses. By the 1990s 350 new golf courses were being built annually. Golf courses use vast amounts of land and there have been many reported cases of land being taken forcibly from local farmers who received little or no compensation. In addition, golf courses use vast amounts of water. In 2004 the WWF estimated that 10–15,000 cubic metres of water per hectare were pumped out of fresh water supplies to golf courses in South East Spain. One golf course could supply a town of 12,000 people in the same area with fresh water for a year. In the Indonesian island of Bali, the average golf course uses 3 million litres of water per day compared to the 200 litres available to each Balinese citizen. In addition, large amounts of artificial fertilizer, pesticides and herbicides are used on golf courses. Much of these will get washed into ground water supplies causing contamination of fresh water supplies. One of the most controversial golf course development occurred in Cyprus when the government authorised the building of 14 new golf courses in 2009. Water is already rationed in the island due to scarce water supplies and low annual rainfall. Locals fear that these golf courses will turn the drought stricken island into a desert in the summer months. To reduce pressure on scarce water resources each golf course will have its own desalination plant so that sea water can be used. However, this will in turn put extra demands on electricity supplies on the island.

In some poorer countries local people have been evicted or displaced from their homes in the interests of maximising tourist potential. Tourism Concern, a voluntary organisation that seeks to protect the human rights of local people against major tourist developers, recently highlighted the displacement of slum dwellers in South Africa. It is claimed that the South African government pursued a policy of 'beautification' ahead of the 2010 World Cup Football competition. 'Beautification' involves clearing slum housing that might deter tourists. It was estimated that close to 500,000 people would attend the World Cup and many more would come as tourists. Thousands of people were to be removed to temporary camps out of sight of the tourists. These temporary camps were a considerable distance from work places, schools and other services.

Many indigenous groups have been forcibly displaced from their traditional lands in order to facilitate tourist developments. There are examples of governments and tourist developers moving tribal peoples from their lands in Kenya, Peru, Thailand and Honduras. Governments and tourist developers have argued that much of this displacement was necessary in the interests

### Additional References

More information is available from Tourism Concern:

www.tourismconcern.org.uk

of conservation and ecotourism but many of those displaced appear to have received little compensation.

It is obvious that the needs of local people have been overlooked in many cases. The problem is really a conflict between the potential wealth that tourist development can bring as opposed to fulfilling the everyday needs of the local community. There are a number of organisations which work to bring some of the worst examples to the public domain. By highlighting the most serious injustices that have occurred these organisations hope to heighten people's moral consciousness against these developments. Recently, a British company planned a 2.8 billion pound tourist development in Zanzibar with luxury hotels, golf courses and an airport. The development threatened the livelihood of some 20,000 local people who feared they might be displaced and lose their valuable agricultural land. Tourism Concern launched a campaign against the company by publishing details of the proposed development in the British press and seeking details of any environmental and social impact assessments carried out by the developers. The campaign was a success and the proposed development was cancelled. The World Tourism Organisation, a United Nations Organisation, sets to promote the sustainable development of tourism throughout the world and encourages the implementation of the aims and objectives of the Millennium Development Goals in tourism development in LEDCs.

## Social Sustainability

Social sustainability refers to the ability of a community to function and adapt to changing situations without having their attitudes and ways of life altered in an adverse manner. Tourists introduce an additional layer of cultural diversity to a region. In some ways this can be an enriching experience but on other occasions it can result in new challenges. Traditional occupations are often abandoned in favour of higher paid opportunities in the service sector in the tourist resorts. Young people in particular will leave rural farming communities to find employment in hotels, cafes and other services. This can have a positive impact in the rural areas if money is sent back to the rural communities in much the same way as migrants often send remittances back home. However, many of the jobs associated with tourism are seasonal and the tourism employee may have no income for part of the year. In addition, much of the work is low paid. In recent times tour companies have been anxious to keep costs low in the face of rising fuel prices and this has resulted in wage levels remaining low. Because wage levels are already low in many of the tourist regions and the supply of labour is abundant, tour companies offer wages that can be as much as 20% lower than in other sectors of industry. There are also limited opportunities for skills development or promotion. Workers often find that because of the seasonal nature of their employment they have to work long and anti-social hours for several months of the year. It has also been shown that this type of work often leads to the break up of families. As much of the tourist trade is in the hands of MNCs (Multi-National Companies), a lot of the money generated from tourism stays in the hands of the MNCs and does not benefit the local community. This process is referred to as **leakage**.

Cultural conflicts can often arise from international tourism. This is especially the case where the more relaxed attitudes of modern tourists towards dress code and alcohol are at odds with more conservative local attitudes in the tourist destination. Potential cultural conflicts exist in some Middle Eastern countries and tourist resorts have even come under attack by those opposed to western cultures in Egypt. In Kenya much of the tourist trade is focused on the wildlife reserves and the Masai tribes. The Masai are tribal pastoralists viewed both as an asset and a threat to tourist development by the Kenyan government. Their traditional lifestyles and customs were regarded as a potential attraction for tourists but their nomadic lifestyle meant they herded their animals on the protected wildlife reserves and they were resettled outside these protected areas. This inevitably caused difficulties for the Masai, leading many to abandon their traditional way of life and become involved in the provision of services such as craft centres. Tourism has brought increased wealth to these areas but overall the lifestyle of the Masai has been changed and younger members are unlikely to keep up the traditional way of life.

The display of wealth by international tourists often attracts numbers of unemployed people searching for employment. This can lead to unscrupulous individuals exploiting these people. On occasions where no work is available women and children often end up in prostitution. More than one million children are sexually abused by tourists every year within the global child sex tourism industry. Although there are a number of organisations working on this issue, the numbers involved in child sex tourism are increasing. In Vietnam, a child's services can be sold for as little as £3, with the trafficking of child sex workers becoming increasingly popular.

Management strategies to deal with some of the issues raised here usually rely on international agreements formulated by bodies such as the UN or through NGOs such as Tourism Concern. The World Tourism Organisation has drawn up a code of ethics for tourism and although the code is not legally binding countries are encouraged to adhere to its recommendations. Tourism Concern has also produced documents relating to serious infringements on human rights including child prostitution and human trafficking. The EU set up The European Trade Union Liaison Committee on Tourism in 1995 to represent workers in the tourism sector. This organisation is mainly concerned with the promotion of sustainable employment in the tourism sector.

## CASE STUDY: Tourism Change and Management in Mallorca

### Growth of Tourism in Mallorca

The island of Mallorca is the largest of the Balearic Islands lying off the east coast of Spain. It enjoys a Mediterranean climate characterised by hot dry summers and mild winters. The island has been a tourist attraction since the mid nineteenth century when wealthy tourists from northern Europe, including Chopin (nineteenth century) and Picasso (twentieth century) visited the island, mostly during the winter months. The numbers involved were quite low. Some purchased second homes but their overall impact on Mallorca was limited and it was not until the 1960s that mass tourism began on the island. In contrast to the earlier tourist developments this led to very significant changes on Mallorca.

Mallorca was one of the earliest European destinations to experience mass tourism, with its mild climate, many high quality beaches and stunning scenery. It is an extremely popular tourist destination, especially with northern Europeans, millions of whom visit Mallorca every year and, during the most popular months, outnumber the resident population three to one. During the 1960s, the demand for foreign holidays increased as a result of the improvements in living standards and the introduction of paid holiday periods in north Western Europe. Package holidays facilitated large numbers of people to consider a holiday outside their own country. The value of Spanish currency in the 1960s (peseta) was relatively low compared to other European currencies, making holidays to Spain in general relatively cheap. Mallorca, with its early experience in the tourist trade, therefore became a popular destination.

The growth in numbers visiting the island was phenomenal. In 1960 400,000 tourists arrived in Mallorca, by 1973 the figures had reached 3.5 million and in 2008 the figure was 8 million. Most of this tourist development was centred around the coastal areas and in particular in the region of Calvia in the south-west of the island. Calvia became one of the most important tourist regions in Mallorca. Annually some 1.7 million tourists visit the resorts of Magaluf, Palma Nova, Santa Ponsa and Peguera. Calvia, with a local population of 44,000, was well suited to the development of mass tourism with almost 60 km of beaches and its close proximity to the international airport at Palma. In the traditional low income farming economy of Mallorca

**Resource 45**   *Palma in Mallorca*

the prospect of better paid jobs in the hotels and other tourist facilities was welcomed by most. There was a rapid increase in the number of hotels to cope with the growing numbers of tourists. Little regard was given to the long term impact on the environment or indeed the quality of the tourist experience. Mass tourism had arrived in Mallorca.

## Consequences of Tourism Growth in Mallorca

Tourism brought an immediate boost to the economy of Mallorca with almost two thirds of its population of 800,000 employed, either directly (in hotels and restaurants) or indirectly (services such as estate agents and food processing), in tourism.

Overall some 84% of Mallorca's Gross National Income (GNI) is connected to tourism. Practically all of the earliest tourist developments were on the coastal region and large numbers of the young, economically active population moved from the rural interior to find seasonal employment in the tourist areas. At the height of the mass tourism boom in Calvia unemployment rates were typically about 4% lower than any other region in Spain and the average family income was 30% above the national average for all of Spain. A massive building programme, including hotels, roads and other amenities for the tourist began providing further opportunities for employment.

The advent of mass tourism did have some economic disadvantages for Mallorca. Some of these developments were financed and designed by international tour operators leaving only semi-skilled and manual job opportunities for the local Mallorcan population. In addition the work in the service sector offered little opportunity for promotion or career advancement. Much of the work provided was seasonal and workers had to work long and anti-social hours to compensate for this seasonality of employment. However, in the early days of mass tourism these disadvantages seemed to be outweighed by the overall economic benefits tourism had brought to the island.

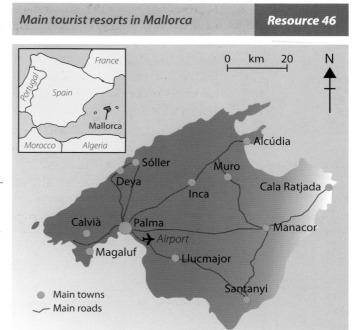

**Main tourist resorts in Mallorca**    **Resource 46**

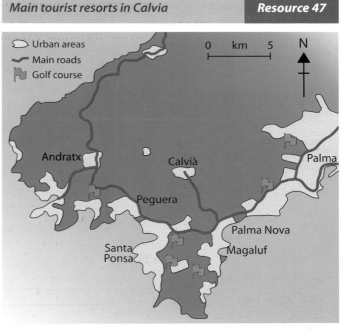

**Main tourist resorts in Calvia**    **Resource 47**

Mass tourism continued unabated well into the late 1970s, by which time the southern part of the island was almost completely transformed. The coastal area of Calvia was densely packed with hotel and apartment complexes, numerous bars, restaurants and other leisure services. A number of English, Irish and German owned bars and restaurants were established to serve the large number of tourists from these countries. In the main tourist resorts most of the restaurants served either English or German food. English was spoken in practically all establishments and it was not necessary for the tourists to speak any Spanish while on holiday in Mallorca. By the late 1970s there was very little traditional Spanish architecture or culture still remaining in this coastal region. Throughout the 1970s and 1980s the island continued to attract large numbers of young people staying in low priced accommodation. Mallorca had acquired a negative image of packed beaches, rowdy bars and nightclubs. Furthermore, the pressure of numbers put undue stress on already inadequate waste disposal systems and the coastal waters were polluted.

It seemed as if mass tourism was effectively destroying the tourist potential in Mallorca. However, there were also serious environmental problems associated with uncontrolled tourism. The seasonal influx of tourists made heavy demands on scarce water resources. The landscaping of gardens within hotel complexes, the building of golf courses, swimming pools and the provision of showers meant that fresh water supplies were being over used. Mallorca had to undertake expensive desalinisation of seawater to meet the demand. In the late 1970s much of the tap water was unfit for drinking. The situation was worse for local people who found it difficult to compete for water supplies against the demands of tourism development. Local residents became increasingly resentful of the creation of golf courses, which used vast amounts of water.

The natural coastal landscape was altered dramatically. In Calvia, beaches were extended by up to 13% in a twenty year period and sand dunes removed to make way for more apartment blocks. Most of the natural dune vegetation was completely destroyed along with their wildlife habitats. In addition, the traditional way of life in Mallorca was affected. Farmers often sold their land to developers who built out of character villas on former agricultural land. Within the tourist centres the landscape was completely altered to provide promenades and other tourist amenities. The increased number of tour buses and other vehicles resulted in an increase in air pollution.

| Resource 48 | *Tourism in Mallorca* |

Packed beach Mallorca

Magaluf Mallorca

An overcrowded built up area in Santa Ponsa

English Café in Magaluf Mallorca

Mallorca faced an impending crisis in the late 1980s. In the Calvia region tourist numbers fell by almost 20% between 1988 and 1991. In part this decrease was due to the rise in the importance of other tourist destinations, such as Florida and the Caribbean. However, it was also due to the decline in the quality of the tourism product offered in Mallorca. These changes in tourism demand highlighted the lack of sustainability in the way tourism had developed in Mallorca. The over reliance on tourism as a major source of income and employment meant that local residents faced an increase in unemployment and a fall in living standards. It was clear that an ambitious management plan was needed if Mallorca was to maintain its importance as a major tourist destination.

## Tourism Management in Mallorca

Mallorca forms part of The Balearic Autonomous Community (BAC), which means it has considerable power over management of its own budget and planning. There had been a number of earlier attempts to deal with the pollution issues in the sea, such as the Action Plan for the Mediterranean (MAP) in the 1970s, but these had limited effects. In 1984, the BAC formulated a plan of action to restore the tourism potential of the islands. There were three main aims:

### 1. Protecting the Environment

- No new building was permitted on a belt of at least 100 m from the coast. Prior to this hotels were often constructed on the site of former beach dunes.
- A number of areas deemed to have fragile ecosystems were given protected land status. Mallorca's first natural park was created in 1988 at Albufera close to Alcudia in the north of the island. It became a Ramsar Site a year later. The Archipelago of Cabrera off the south-east coast became a National Park in 1993.
- Increased restrictions were introduced on the building of villas and second homes in rural areas.

### 2. Limiting the Growth of Tourism

- Planning restrictions on the density of tourist accommodation were introduced by doubling the amount of land available per tourism bed from 30 m$^2$ to 60 m$^2$.
- Mallorca participated in the ECOMOST project, which was a research group involving international tour operators and local developers seeking to establish more sustainable tourism across Mediterranean countries.
- An Off Peak Tourism Season Plan was initiated in an attempt to diversify tourism provision and to overcome the problem of seasonal employment.

### 3. Improving the Tourism Product, Service and Infrastructure

- US$200,000,000 was invested in a new waste disposal system to reduce the threat of pollution of coastal areas. As a result many of Mallorca's beaches have now been awarded 'Blue Flag' status by the European Union.
- A Plan to Embellish Tourism Resorts was introduced. This involved improving sea promenades, new street lighting and green zones.
- An ambitious modernisation plan for all tourist accommodation built before 1984. Hotels that did not comply with this regulation could be forced to close.
- Measures were put in place to preserve the Mallorcan identity within rural towns and villages away from the coast. At the same time these inland areas were encouraged to engage in small rural tourism projects.

### Local Agenda 21 in Calvia

The Calvia region formulated its own tourism plan as part of a Local Agenda 21 programme for sustainability. More information on Local Agenda 21 is available from *A2 Geography For CCEA* (Colourpoint, 2009), page 65. As one of the first areas to develop mass tourism in Mallorca, Calvia suffered most from over development. This project sought to make tourism more sustainable through a number of initiatives including:

- reducing the number of tourists but up grading the quality of tourism in order to attract a higher spending clientele.
- the demolition of five sea front hotels and converting the land into green areas. In addition, all new building must adhere to strict planning restrictions and regulations regarding density of occupancy, waste disposal and energy conservation.
- schemes to direct tourism away from the coast into activities such as hill walking, cycling and golfing.
- an ambitious coastal scheme to protect fragile landscapes and ecosystems, and repair damage.

---

**Resource 49**    *Sustainable tourism*

---

*Below:* Cycling in Soller, Western Mallorca (location on map, **Resource 46**).

*Left and below:* Redevelopment sites in Calvia.

*Above and below:* Alternative tourism opportunities in Mallorca such as hill walking and cycling.

*Above:* 'Zona Verde' is a green zone. The rest of the notice prohibits littering.

The example of Mallorca aptly demonstrates the changing nature of tourism and its consequences. New locations (Pleasure Periphery, page 46) are popular so long as they meet the tourists' demands. Over time, new destinations compete with the established resorts which then face a decrease in popularity (Product Cycle, page 47) Mallorca also illustrates how management schemes can rejuvenate a declining tourist resort (Butler Model, page 48) and achieve a more sustainable form of tourist development. One of the key issues was overcrowding on beaches and in hotel development. The management response was to examine the carrying capacity of the region and reduce tourist densities (Carrying Capacity, page 50–51 and Limits of Acceptable Change, page 52). The earliest tourist sites were largely concentrated in the south but now the entire island is engaged with the tourist trade. In addition, most of the new developments have been carried out by the Mallorcan Authorities and in the Calvia region there is considerable involvement of the local people in the decision making process. This stands in marked contrast to some of the earliest developments that were largely associated with the international tour operators. In 2009, tourism remains the most important source of income in Mallorca. The traditional coastal areas are still crowded in the summer season but there is now a greater variety of tourism products on offer, the tourist season has been widened and the principles of sustainability are considered in all aspects of management.

**Additional References**

S'Albufera de Mallorca – www.mallorcaweb.net/salbufera/introang.html

Map of Mallorca – www.mallorcaweb.com/map-mallorca/

Calvia – www.calvia.com/

# ECOTOURISM

The problems discussed in the Case Study of Mallorca (pages 56–61) in relation to mass tourism clearly illustrate the importance of management policies if sustainability is to be maintained. In the 1990s a new type of tourism development, known as 'ecotourism', emerged that claimed to accentuate the positive returns of tourism whilst minimising the negative outcomes of mass tourism. Ecotourism is defined by The International Ecotourism Society (TIES) as "responsible travel to fragile and usually protected areas where the funds are used for economic and social development of local communities." Tropical rainforests with their delicate ecosystems, tropical grasslands and wilderness areas, such as Alaska, are among the best known examples of ecotourism. According to TIES there are seven characteristics of ecotourism:

- Involves travel to natural destinations.
- Minimises impact on the natural environment.
- Builds environmental awareness.
- Provides financial benefits for conservation.
- Provides financial benefits and empowerment for local people.
- Respects local culture.
- Supports human rights and demographic movements.

## Growth of Ecotourism

The number of ecotourism trips has been increasing at a rate of 20% annually over the last decade, almost three times faster than the tourist industry as a whole. It is claimed that the sun and sand resort tourism has reached its peak and other types of holiday, including ecotourism, are growing. The technological developments in air transport that facilitated mass tourism have also enabled people to travel further afield. Increased knowledge of the world has led people to visit areas for a specific interest – the so-called 'niche tourism'. Ecotourism is one example of niche tourism and it represents a new level in the pleasure periphery model. There are two basic considerations underlying ecotourism development:

1. The main attraction to an ecotourism destination is the natural or semi-natural ecosystem. It is therefore crucial for all ecotourism destinations to include a conservation plan to protect this ecosystem. If the ecosystem is damaged there is nothing to attract the tourists.
2. Ecotourists are looking for a real experience of the wilderness area they are visiting and will be deterred by large numbers of other tourists.

Both of these considerations mean that the carrying capacity is usually quite low for all ecotourist destinations. Many ecotourism sites are in LEDCs and they stand to benefit considerably from such developments. In Costa Rica, ecotourism provides employment for 140,000 local people and contributes 17% of the country's GNI. It is also claimed that ecotourists spend more per capita than the mass tourist (**Resource 50**).

## Tourist Spending – Ecotourism vs Mass Tourism

- In Dominica, in the Caribbean, ecotourists using small, nature-based lodges spent 18 times more than cruise passengers spent while visiting the island.
- In Komodo National Park in Indonesia, independent travelers spend nearly US$100 locally per visit; package holidaymakers spend only half this.
- 80% of money for all-inclusive package tours goes to airlines, hotels, and other international companies. Eco-lodges hire and purchase locally, and sometimes put as much as 95% of money into the local economy.
- The daily expenditure of cultural tourists (over €70/£58) is higher than beach holiday tourists (€48/£40).

There are an estimated 5 million ecotourists annually, mostly from USA, Western Europe, Canada and Australia.

Eco-lodge and white water rafting in Belize, Central America

## Profile of Ecotourists

- Experienced travelers
- Higher education
- Higher income bracket
- Middle-aged to elderly
- Opinion leaders
- Ask and tell their friends and colleagues about trip
- Are the most important source of trip information

Source: TIES Global Ecotourism Fact sheet (pages 3–4), The International Ecotourism Society, www.ecotourism.org

## Ecotoursim – Good or Bad?

Few aspects of tourism have attracted the level of debate that surrounds ecotourism. On the one hand it is viewed by many as an excellent economic opportunity, particularly for LEDCs, but for others ecotourism threatens fragile environments and contributes little to the local population. Currently there are no internationally agreed criteria for ecotourism accreditation and this is a major issue. Critics claim that the concept of ecotourism is loosely interpreted to include any tourist project that is related to the natural environment. There are examples of international tour operators placing luxurious hotels in tropical areas, paying token attention to the ideals of ecotourism and claiming these resorts as eco-friendly. Such practices are referred to as '**greenwashing**'. This is an extreme case but even those developments that do adhere more strongly to the principles of ecotourism have attracted serious criticism. There is no definitive answer to the question: is ecotourism good or bad? A number of examples are included here to highlight some of the issues involved.

### Ecotourism in Costa Rica

The Caribbean island of Costa Rica has a tropical climate, a wealth of biodiversity in the rain forest areas as well as volcanic landscapes, beaches and off shore coral reefs. A National Park Service was established in the 1970s to manage these diverse environments and over 25% of the island has some form of protected status. With such a wide range of environments and a relatively high standard of living for a LEDC, the island was well suited to the development of tourism and attracted large numbers of wealthy tourists from the USA. The Costa Rican Government was anxious to develop tourism that would bring economic benefits but also conserve the environmental wealth of the island. Many believe that Costa Rica pioneered the concept of ecotourism.

The first ecotourism developments involved eco-lodges. Eco-lodges are groups of small huts built in clearings in the forest using wood that had been discarded by loggers. The eco-lodges are quite basic by western standards, with no electricity. Biodegradable soaps are used for washing and all glass and plastic is recycled. Water is purified by using naturally occurring enzymes and bacteria, and heated by solar energy. The owners of the eco-lodges are Costa Rican and they have set up a charitable trust to educate people about the rainforest and provide

| Resource 51 | Costa Rica Ecotourism |

Hanging bridge in the Monteverde Cloudforest Reserve, Costa Rica. Tourists walk above the forest, preventing them from damaging the vegetation or wildlife habitats below.

Bird watching in Corcovado National Park, Costa Rica. Is this really ecotourism?

activities such as bird watching. Initially, the eco-lodges had no luxuries but over time the facilities have been upgraded to meet tourist demand. There is now a range of accommodation available from the very basic to the world's most expensive and opulent, owned by Americans. These more expensive lodges still use local materials and employ local people as guides, waiters and cleaners. However, as these are foreign owned developments much of the profit raised is returned to the owners and the low paid jobs are the only benefits to the local community.

In the last ten years Costa Rica has faced competition from other countries involved in ecotourism. In order to maintain their competitive edge Costa Rica has diversified into eco-adventure holidays. These include zip wires through the rain forest canopy, white water rafting, mountain biking and hiking through the forest. These types of activity have attracted a higher spending tourist and the economic opportunities for locals are increasing through the greater demand for services and instructors.

Costa Rica has benefited enormously from these developments. About 75% of the hotels are still locally owned and large numbers of people have found employment as a result of these developments. Nevertheless, there have been criticisms. Many young Costa Ricans left work in farming to find better paid work in tourism. Consequently, agriculture declined and Costa Rica now imports food. As already stated, some of the largest and most expensive lodges or hotels are owned by outsiders and as result profit made from tourism goes back to the owners. In addition, these foreign owned hotels are deemed to be lax in their adherence to the ethics of ecotourism. There are also issues regarding waste disposal in landfill sites. The increase in the number of vehicles associated with the tourist resorts is contributing to air pollution, while some of the new adventure tourism threatens wildlife habitats. Tourists feeding animals has created problems, as animals are not feeding on their natural diet. The dilemma for Costa Rica in the future is how to maintain the balance between economic gain and environmental conservation.

## Ecotourism in Belize

Belize is another country in the Caribbean where ecotourism has been developed. However, the outcome has been less successful than in Costa Rica. The country has many obvious attractions for ecotourism including an off shore coral barrier reef, over 450 low lying islands, a wealth

**Ecotourism Attractions in Belize**                                    *Resource 52*

Mayan ruins and mangrove swamps, Belize

of wildlife and antiquities of the ancient Mayan civilisations. The country has approximately 25% of its territory designated as protected land in some form. Like Costa Rica it is in close proximity to the wealthy tourist market of the USA. From the beginning Belize concentrated on the elite tourist market and this may explain some of the conflicts experienced in the country regarding ecotourism. Whist there are some locally controlled projects over 90% of recent developments are large-scale luxury hotels owned by international companies. There are also serious environmental degradation issues including:

- Mangrove swamps have been drained to make way for a landing strip, destroying important nesting grounds for birds.
- The coral reef has been damaged and there is over fishing, leading to a decline in lobster numbers.
- Unsupervised groups of tourists are permitted to visit nature reserves and they often fail to take sufficient care of the environment.

### Displacement of people and threats to indigenous cultures in Kenya

Displacement of people is one of the most controversial negative aspects of ecotourism developments. In Kenya, the Masai Mara wildlife reserve attracts large numbers of ecotourists annually. Over 70% of these wildlife reserves are lands occupied by the Masai, a group of nomadic pastoralists. They have been denied access to grazing land in the protected areas, putting their only livelihood at risk. The Masai have not been compensated for this loss of livelihood and they have been unable to gain employment in the reserves, as most of the jobs go to better educated workers. Furthermore, the investors in this area are not local and have not put profits back into local economy. In some cases game reserves were created without informing or consulting local people, who only found out about the situation when they received an eviction notice.

The Masai traditional way of life is under threat from ecotourism in other ways. The Masai people are viewed as a 'backdrop' to the ecotourist experience and many feel exploited as they are photographed by wealthy western visitors. The presence of affluent ecotourists has also encouraged the development of markets in wildlife souvenirs. Such practices are at odds with conservation policies and are happening in many other destinations worldwide.

| Resource 53 | *The Masai people, Kenya* |

Masai people in traditional dress

The Masai people are viewed as a 'backdrop' to the ecotourist experience and are often photographed by tourists.

# Ecotourism regulation

In countries where ecotourism is a major source of income governments are often lured more by short economic gain than long-term environmental protection. There are issues and conflicts relating to the allocation of resources in many areas. Although ecotourist destinations generally cater for relatively small numbers of people, this can put undue demands on limited infrastructure. Water treatment plants and sanitation facilities all require land and this often means forest clearance. The conversion of natural land to tourist infrastructure is thought to have contributed to habitat damage for squirrel monkeys in Costa Rica. There are many reported cases in some East African ecotourist sites of waste being dumped directly into rivers because of lack of available waste disposal systems. This has led to contamination of river water making it unfit for use by local people. Western ecotourists make much greater demands on resources than local people in LEDCs.

**Ecotourism regulation**

**Resource 54**

Tour guides are encouraged by the promise of lucrative 'tips' from the tourists to divert from permitted trails in the hope of gaining better views of wildlife. Such activities can frighten animals away from these paths, leading to disruption of their feeding and nesting sites.

Guided tours through fragile environments to observe wildlife can pose a serious threat to natural habitats, as well as contributing to soil compaction and plant damage. Tour guides have been encouraged by the promise of lucrative 'tips' from the tourists to divert from permitted trails in the hope of gaining better views of wildlife. Such activities can frighten animals away from these paths, leading to disruption of their feeding and nesting sites.

Where ecotourism has been developed by foreign companies the threat of profit leakage deprives the local community of much needed revenue. In Nepal, over 90% of ecotourism profits are returned or leaked to foreign countries and less than 5% is used for local community projects.

The examples noted here illustrate the need for some form of international regulation for ecotourism. A 'Green Stars' scheme has been suggested for all new ecotourist developments. This would entail the production of a draft plan giving details of a proposed scheme as well as details of the potential benefits to the local community in terms of education and staff training. The plan would also carry out an environmental impact assessment exercise and use this to plan for infrastructure requirements and set a tourist capacity limit. As yet there has been no international agreement to enforce any one scheme and individual countries are free to set their own requirements for ecotourism developments. Until some form of agreement is reached ecotourism will remain loosely interpreted and the conflicts over economic and environmental issues will continue.

**Figure 1**

## Visiting disaster

**A rapid growth in ecotourism has been made at the expense of indigenous peoples around the world.**

[In 2002] 250 Filipinos were evicted from their homes. Their lakeshore village of Ambulong, in Batangas province, was attacked by hundreds of police, who demolished 24 houses. Many people were reported wounded ... The intention of the authorities was to clear people to make way for a major business venture – not oil, logging or mining, but ecotourism, which is growing massively around the world and is now backed by governments, world bodies and international banks. The United Nations has declared 2002 the international year of ecotourism, and last month a world summit was held in Canada to consider the problems and potential for the fastest growing sector of the world's largest industry. According to many conservationists and tour operators, this "benign" version of tourism offers a way to fund environmental protection, stimulate the incomes of the poor and encourage cultural exchange ... Ecuador earns more than $100 m a year from 60,000 visitors to the Galapagos, for instance, and Kenya as much income from its safari holidays. While ecotourism run by indigenous communities can be a lifesaver in areas where other income sources are being depleted, all too often these very people are being left out of the ecotourism development plans. The dispossession of people from their land is increasingly associated with ecotourism.

The cases are widespread. In the Moulvibaza district of Bangladesh more than 1,000 families of the Khasi and Garoare indigenous groups face eviction from their ancestral lands for the development of a 610 hectare eco-park ... In Brazil two fishing villages near the coastal resort town of Fortaleza are fighting for their land. In one, Tatajuba, recently voted one of the world's top 10 beach sites by the Washington Post, a village of 150 families has gone to court to try to show that a real estate agency illegally took possession of publicly protected land where they live. A company wants to build a 5,000-hectare "ecological resort catering for 1,500 tourists" in their place. In Prainha do Canto Verde, a village of 1,100 families, the community is also defending itself against speculators who, they say, bought beach land deceptively from fishing families and then registered the land for clearance. "It wasn't illegal, but the fishing families can't read and didn't know what was happening," says Rene Schaerer, a United States public policy adviser working with the community.

Governments in developing countries, keen to modernise, often say that "primitive" subsistence activities are incompatible with conservation. These were the arguments given to evict the Masai in East Africa and the Bushmen of Botswana, but the reality is that many indigenous and other poor communities are living on prime areas of ecotourism real estate and speculators want the land. Much ecotourism development comes as part of "development packages" funded by international banks ... The Inter-American Development Bank has been the focus of protest by the Tatajuba and Prainha do Canto communities ...

Few poor communities are set against ecotourism, but they almost all want to be able to control it. "We were about to start community ecotourism on our lands, as bushmen in Namibia have done," said a Khwe bushman in Botswana. "But then the intimidation, torture and evictions started again. The government did not want to lose tourism business to us." ... Deborah McLaren, a native American with [a] Rethinking Tourism Project [says] "Communities are being oppressed. Governments and industry have corrupted the whole idea of ecotourism, and it is proving just as destructive as any other industry. But somehow, no one wants to hear that."

*By Sue Wheat, 'Visiting Disaster', The Guardian, 20 June 2002,*
*Copyright Guardian News & Media Ltd 2002*

**Figure 2**

## Tourists join Masai Dancers at Holiday Resort in the Masai Mara

*Source: Nathan Dixey, www.npd-photography.com*

**Figure 3**

## Minivans bringing tourists through the Masai Mara

**Figures 1–3 adapted from resources for CCEA May 2008**

## Exercise

Using all of the information here and additional material from your own research, answer the following question:

Can ecotourism exist?

## Additional References

### Websites

The International Ecotourism Society – www.ecotourism.org/site/

*Exploring Ecotourism*, Planeta.com – www.planeta.com/ecotravel/tour/definitions.html

*Eco and Sustainable Tourism*, The Global Development Research Center –
www.gdrc.org/uem/eco-tour/eco-sust.html

Sustainable Travel International – www.sustainabletravelinternational.org/

Rainforest Alliance – www.rainforest-alliance.org/locations/brazil/tourism.html

*Ecotourism*, Mongabay.com – http://rainforests.mongabay.com/1004.htm

Rainforest Ecotourism – www.rainforestecotourism.com/

Sustainable Tourism – www.sustainabletourism.net/

*Sustainable Tourism*, United Nations – www.un.org/esa/sustdev/natlinfo/indicators/idsd/themes/tourism.htm

*The Economic Impacts of Ecotourism*, Ecotourism – www.ecotourism.ee/oko/kreg.html

Ecotourism Kenya – http://ecotourismkenya.com/

*Ecotourism in Kenya: Campi ya Kanzi*, go nomad.com – www.gonomad.com/lodgings/0705/kenya.html

*Ecotourism in Kenya*, Eco Resorts – www.eco-resorts.com/Archives/ktb-press-release.php

*Ecotourism*, Classic Escapes – www.classicescapes.com/ke-ecotourism.html

*The Best Green Adventures on Earth*, National Geographic –
www.nationalgeographic.com/adventure/travel/eco-travel/index.html

*Sustainable Development of Ecotourism*, World Tourism Organization –
www.world-tourism.org/sustainable/IYE-Main-Menu.htm

*ORTPN in ecotourism drive*, Rwanda Development Gateway –
www.rwandagateway.org/article.php3?id_article=1414

*Ecotourism: an Introduction*, Andean Travel Web – www.andeantravelweb.com/peru/ecotourism/index.html

### Geofile Articles

*Sustainable Management of Fragile Environments*, Geofile online, January 2010 (Nelson Thornes, 2010)

*An Ecotourism Case Study – Costa Rica*, Geofile online, September 2009 (Nelson Thornes, 2009)

### Publications

R Prosser, *Leisure, Recreation and Tourism* (Collins Educational, 2000)

## Tourism in Northern Ireland

Tourism has always been important in Northern Ireland. The province has a long history of emigration and this resulted in return trips to visit family and friends (VFR). In more recent times, with greater political stability, the potential for tourism development has been exploited to the full. Increased air routes by the budget airlines have facilitated international tourist developments. There is a rich variety of landscape and coastline, as well as historic buildings and settlements. In Belfast some of the former sites of bitter sectarian conflict are now part of the tourist sightseeing itinerary on the many guided tours on offer across the city. In a region with limited potential for industrial development, tourism is a major source of revenue.

| Visitor tourism revenue 1998–2008 | Resource 55 |

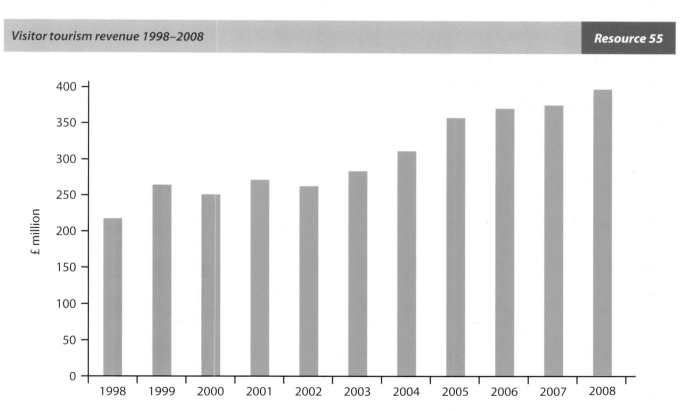

Source: Data from 'Tourism Facts 2008', Northern Ireland Tourist Board, www.nitb.com

**Resource 56**    *Murals*

The murals of Belfast are often part of the city's sightseeing itinerary.

As tourism increases so too does the need for management policies. The Northern Ireland Tourist Board (NITB) is a non-governmental organisation that works with a number of government departments, including the Department of Environment (DOE), to implement tourism management policies. These policies range from the awarding of protected land status such as AONBs to regeneration of historic sites such as Titanic Quarter in Belfast (**Resource 57**).

**Resource 57**

### Work Progressing on £97 million Titanic Signature Building

Tourism Minister Arlene Foster today confirmed that work is progressing well on the £97 million Titanic Signature Building in the heart of the Titanic Quarter, Belfast.

Commenting on the construction work underway, the Minister said: "Good progress is being made to create a truly world class tourist attraction for Northern Ireland. We have a proud industrial and maritime heritage, and only Belfast can tell the complete story of the world famous 'RMS Titanic'. This project will also give potential visitors a unique and compelling reason to choose Northern Ireland as their destination.

"The social and economic benefits will also be very significant. We estimate that the Titanic Signature Building will attract around 400,000 visitors annually, of which between 130,000 and 165,000 will be from outside Northern Ireland.

"The advantages of this project also stretch far beyond tourism. In the current difficult economic climate this project provides an important boost for the construction industry. Furthermore there will be additional economic benefits that will result from a rise in indirect employment in other sectors, due to increased visitor numbers."

*Source:* Work Progressing on £97 million Titanic Building,
*4 December 2009, Northern Ireland Tourist Board, http://www.nitb.com/,*
*accessed 1 March 2010*

Tourism management policies are usually controversial, especially if there is the potential for conflict between different groups of people. A recent controversial issue relates to the possibility of awarding National Park status to the Mournes area **Resource 58**. Such policies impact on local communities and there are plenty of opportunities to investigate attitudes towards these proposed developments. It is important to remember that attitudes vary between different groups of people. In the Mournes area, local residents and farmers are known to have different attitudes towards the proposed National Park than local shopkeepers. Sustainable tourism measures have also been incorporated in many areas across Northern Ireland and attitudes towards these could form the basis of an investigation. Alternatively, the physical and environmental impacts of tourism could be investigated at a honeypot site. Information on possible fieldwork measurements of footpath erosion, vegetation trampling and soil infiltration rates is available in *Geofile* online, September 2004 (Nelson Thornes 2004). An environmental quality survey can be carried out at a number of locations using a bi-polar matrix as shown in the **Exercise on page 74**. An environmental quality survey in tourism is a means of assessing the tourist attraction of a tourist resort. A bi-polar matrix has two pairs of words at opposite ends of a scale. A numerical score is awarded from 1–5 based on your assessment of each category. A high score reflects good tourist attraction while a low score reflects a negative assessment. The total values are then calculated. In this way a number of locations can be compared. In this example descriptions for the highest and lowest values only are given. As part of your preparation to collect primary data for your investigation the intervening values will need to be decided.

*The Mournes*                                                                 *Resource 58*

The possibility of awarding National Park status to the Mournes has proved a controversial issue.

**Exercise**

## Bi-polar matrix

Use the bi-polar matrix below to measure the attractiveness of your chosen honey pot site.

Date: _____     Time: _____     Weather: _____

| | 1 | 2 | 3 | 4 | 5 | |
|---|---|---|---|---|---|---|
| Noisy | | | | | | Peaceful |
| Unattractive scenery | | | | | | Attractive scenery |
| Lots of litter | | | | | | No litter |
| Poor Visitor information (no signs, leaflets, etc) | | | | | | Good Visitor information (many signs, leaflets, etc) |
| Overcrowded | | | | | | Good balance of people and space |
| No natural habitat | | | | | | Natural habitat |
| Path erosion | | | | | | No path erosion |
| Unattractive buildings | | | | | | Attractive buildings |
| Poor visitor facilities (no toilets, bins, shops, cafes) | | | | | | Good visitor facilities (lots of toilets, bins, shops) |

Source: 'Fieldwork', Geography Teaching Today, http://www.geographyteachingtoday.org.uk/fieldwork/

## Additional References

Information on protected land in Northern Ireland can be found on the Northern Ireland Environment Agency website – www.ni-environment.gov.uk/

The Northern Ireland Tourist Board website provides information on major tourist developments within Northern Ireland and provides links to other sources of background information – www.nitb.com/

Information on ecotourism in Northern Ireland can be found on the Discover Northern Ireland website – www.discovernorthernireland.com/ecotourism/

Mourne Heritage Trust – www.mournelive.com/sustainabletourism/topics/index.asp

Causeway Coast and Glens Heritage Trust – www.ccght.org/

The National Trust – www.nationaltrust.org.uk/main/w-global/w-localtoyou/w-northernireland.htm

Tourism in Fermanagh – www.fermanaghlakelands.com/

Tourism in the Sperrins – www.sperrinstourism.com/

# GLOSSARY

## Nuclear Energy

**Americium:** A radioisotope derived from plutonium formed in a nuclear reactor.

**Atmospheric testing:** Testing of nuclear weapons in the atmosphere.

**Back-end:** The part of nuclear power generation involving treatment of wastes during the operation of the nuclear reactor and treatment of the fuel when it is spent (see front-end).

**Becquerel (Bq):** A measure of the rate of radioactive decay; one Becquerel is the equivalent of one atomic disintegration per second.

**Bikini Atoll:** An island in the Marshall Islands in the Pacific Ocean which has been the site of more than 20 nuclear tests.

**BNFL:** British Nuclear Fuels plc is owned by the British Government, which used to manufacture and transport nuclear fuel.

**Caesium-137:** A radioactive isotope of caesium, mainly formed as a product of nuclear fission, with a half-life of just over 30 years.

**Carcinogenic:** A substance that increases the chances of cancer being caused.

**Chernobyl:** A city in Ukraine abandoned after a nuclear explosion in 1986.

**Chronic exposure:** Exposure to something, such as radioactivity, over a long period of time.

**Cold War:** The political conflict and military tension after World War II, primarily between the Soviet Union and the United States (1947–1991).

**Compaction:** Reduction of volume, eg in disposing of radioactive waste.

**Comprehensive Test Ban Treaty:** A treaty which bans all nuclear explosions in all environments, for military or civilian purposes. Adopted by the United Nations General Assembly in 1996, a number of nuclear powers have yet to sign it. It was preceded by the Limited Test ban Treaty.

**Deep burial:** The disposal of radioactive waste in underground chambers, up to 1 km underground.

**Disposal casks:** Containers in which radioactive waste will be stored before it is disposed of.

**DNA:** Deoxyribonucleic acid (DNA) contains all the genetic instructions used by living organisms.

**Fission:** Splitting the nucleus of an atom into smaller parts.

**Front-end:** The part of nuclear power generation involving the mining of uranium to supply fuel for the reactor (see back-end).

**Fuel rods:** Bundles of nuclear fuel used in nuclear reactors.

**Fusion:** The process of atomic nuclei joining together to form a single heavier nucleus, releasing energy in the process.

**G7:** The meeting of the Finance Ministers of seven industrialised countries: France, United Kingdom, Germany, Canada, Italy, United States and Japan.

**Genetic mutations:** Changes to the DNA of a cell, which can be caused by radiation, often causing harmful effects on organisms.

**Greenpeace:** A Non-Governmental Organisation campaigning on environmental issues.

**Half-life:** The period of time it takes for a substance, such as a radioactive atom, to decrease by half, ie the time needed for levels of radioactivity to reduce by half.

**Herbivores:** Animals that feed mainly on plants.

**High-level waste:** Waste created by the reprocessing of spent nuclear fuel with high levels of radioactivity.

**Incineration:** Burning, in this case of low level radwaste, to reduce volume before disposal.

**Iodine:** An element which can be used to treat thyroid cancer.

**Isotope:** Types of atoms, some of which are radioactive.

**Leaching:** The extraction of materials into a liquid, as in the use of sulphuric acid to extract uranium from uranium ore.

**LEDC:** Less Economically Developed Country.

**Leukemia:** Cancer of the blood or bone marrow

**Limited Test Ban Treaty:** A treaty signed in 1963 committing those who signed not to test nuclear weapons, apart from underground. This was superseded by the Comprehensive Test Ban Treaty.

**MEDC:** More Economically Developed Country.

**Millisievert:** Radiation dose measurement. The maximum dose of radiation for the general public should not exceed 1 millisievert (mSv) per year.

**Mox Nuclear Reactors:** Nuclear power plants that use Mixed Oxide (MOX) as fuel. This contains more than one oxide of nuclear material, generally a blend of plutonium and uranium or reprocessed uranium.

**New Safe Confinement (NSC):** The structure planned to cover the remains of the nuclear reactor at Chernobyl, scheduled to be in place in 2012.

**Nuclear energy:** Power generated from controlled nuclear reactions, using nuclear fission to produce electricity.

**Nuclear reactor:** A system that contains controlled nuclear chain reactions.

**Nuclear reprocessing plant:** A facility in which components of spent nuclear fuel are separated. The separated components can be used in creating nuclear weapons, further used in some nuclear reactors or can be sent for storage.

**Nuclear weapon testing:** Experiments used to evaluate the effectiveness of a nuclear weapon.

**Plutonium:** A radioactive chemical element. Plutonium-239 is the most important isotope and has a half-life of 24,100 years.

**Radiation Exposure Compensation Program:** The result of the Radiation Exposure Compensation Act in the USA. This provided compensation for people made ill by nuclear weapons testing, or from working in uranium mines.

**Radioactive:** Unstable atomic nuclei losing energy by emitting radiation.

**Radioactive contamination:** The uncontrolled release of radioactivity in an environment.

**Radioisotope:** A radioactive isotope or an atom with an unstable nucleus.

**Radon:** A radioactive gas which has no colour, smell or taste. It occurs naturally as uranium in rocks decays.

**Radwaste:** Radioactive waste.

**Reprocessing plant:** See Nuclear reprocessing plant.

**Rods:** See Fuel rods.

**Russian Federation:** The largest country in the world, a remnant of the Soviet Union (USSR), which was dissolved in 1991.

**Sarcophagus:** A container for a corpse, usually carved from stone. Used as a nickname for the reinforced concrete container covering the Chernobyl nuclear reactor.

**Sellafield:** A nuclear processing plant which also used to generate electricity on the coast of the Irish Sea in Cumbria, NW England.

**Sievert:** A measure of a radiation dose. 1 sievert is 1,000 times the safe annual dose recommended for members of the general public.

**Slurry:** A thick mixture of solids in a liquid, usually water.

**Spent fuel:** Nuclear fuel from a nuclear reactor which can no longer support a nuclear reaction.

**Spent fuel rods:** Bundles of nuclear fuel used in nuclear reactors which can no longer support a nuclear reaction.

**Strontium:** A highly radioactive chemical element with a half-life of 28.90 years.

**Synroc:** A term made from the phrase 'synthetic rock', developed to store radioactive waste.

**Tailings:** The materials left over after the useful parts of an ore have been removed.

**Thyroid cancer:** Malignant disease of the thyroid gland, treated with radioactive iodine.

**Thyroid gland:** A gland found in the neck.

**Underground testing:** Nuclear weapon testing under the surface of the earth.

**Underwater testing:** Nuclear weapon testing under water, often suspended from a ship.

**United Nations:** An international organisation founded after World War II. Its aim is to stop wars between countries, and to promote economic and social development.

**Uranium:** A chemical element with low levels of radioactivity. Uranium-238 has a half-life of 4.47 billion years.

**Uranium processing mills:** The grinding of uranium ore to create a uniform size of particle before being treated by chemicals to extract the uranium.

**Vitrification:** Transforming nuclear waste by incorporating it into glass.

## Issues in Tourism

**Adventure tourism:** Tourism involving a sense of adventure, often to places like the Himalayas or Antarctica.

**AONB (Area of Outstanding Natural Beauty):** An area of countryside in England, Wales or Northern Ireland deemed to have significant landscape value.

**ASSI (Area of Specific Scientific Interest):** An area of land deemed by scientific survey as being of the highest degree of conservation value.

**Butler Model:** Devised to examine the evolution of a tourist resort over time, the Butler Model is a refinement of the Product Cycle Model, incorporating the possibility of human intervention through management policies. There are six stages in this model: exploration, involvement, development, consolidation, stagnation, decline/rejuvenation.

**Carrying capacity:** The maximum number of tourists that can be comfortably supported in a resort. If at this maximum, an increase in tourist numbers would adversely affect the tourist potential of the area.

**Ecotourism:** Environmentally friendly or green tourism.

**Greenwashing:** International tour operators placing luxurious hotels in tropical areas, paying token attention to the ideals of ecotourism and claiming these resorts as eco-friendly.

**Honeypot sites:** Areas that attract large numbers of tourists, often leading to overcrowding.

**International tourist arrivals, incoming tourists or inbound tourists:** International tourists in their destination country.

**Leakage:** This usually occurs in LEDCs, where foreign companies develop tourism and claim the profits. The profits are therefore of no benefit to the local community.

**Limits of Acceptable Change (LAC):** A method of assessing the effects of increased tourist numbers on the quality of visitor experience in a resort or tourist region.

**Mass tourism:** Where a large number of tourists are concentrated in a few well developed holiday resorts.

**Niche tourism:** Visiting areas for a specific interest.

**Outbound tourists:** Tourists leaving their home country to go abroad on holiday.

**Package holiday:** An 'all in' deal for tourists whereby a travel company arranges all aspects of the holiday from flights, accommodation, transport to and from the holiday airport, and offers tours and activities to the tourist.

**Pleasure Periphery:** A tourism model that focuses on the behavioural demands of the tourist over time. Tourism is envisaged as a 'fashion industry' where tourists want to spend their holidays in the new and more fashionable resorts. The boundaries of tourism are seen as a tidal wave spreading outwards from the tourists' home area.

**Product Cycle:** A tourism model that examines the evolution of a tourist resort over time. The product cycle model compares tourism to the exploitation of a finite resource. If the resort is over developed it will go into decline. This model can be used to show evolution of a single tourist resort in time or it can locate different resorts on the model at one specific time period.

**Pollution:** Pollution is the introduction of harmful substances into an environment. In the case of tourism this includes increased litter, waste and noise, disposal issues and damaged landscapes, all resulting from tourist developments. Pollution is one of the main negative impacts of tourism.

**Social sustainability:** The ability of a community to function and adapt to changing situations without having their attitudes and ways of life altered in an adverse manner.

**Theme park:** An amusement park or resort developed around a theme, with the buildings and rides reflecting this. Examples include Euro Disney (Paris, France), Alton Towers (Staffordshire, England) and Six Flags (New Jersey, US).

**Visiting Friends and Relatives (VFR):** An important reason for tourism growth is individuals wishing to spend time with friends and family.

## Copyright Information

Copyright has been acknowledged to the best of our ability. If there are any inadvertent errors or omissions, we shall be happy to correct them in any future editions.

The following questions and resources are included with the permission of the Northern Ireland Council for the Curriculum, Examinations and Assessment.

CCEA, GCE A2-1 and A2-2 Geography Compendium © 2005-2009, © 2007-2010

Pages 17 (Resource 7), 32 (Figure 1), 33 (Figure 2, Questions 1&2), 39 (Question 2), 53 (Resource 41, Question 2), 68 (Figures 1–3)

GCE Geography, Assessment Unit A2 1 Human Interaction and Global issues (AG211), CCEA 2010

Pages 13 (Questions 1&2), 37 (Questions 1&2), 39 (Questions 1&3)

GCE Teacher Guidance, Geography A2 1 Human Geography and Global Issues, Section B Global Issues: Guidance on the Delivery of Fieldwork at A2, CCEA, 2009

Pages 7 (flowchart diagram), 8 (text)

Figures 1 and 2 on pages 32 and 33 are licensed by Colourpoint Books from *The Independent* for republication in this book. Figure 1 © 2006 Independent Print Limited; Figure 2 © 2005 Independent Print Limited. All rights reserved.

Resource 41 on page 53 is included with the permission of NI Syndication, © *The Sunday Times - March 2002 / nisyndication.com*. A copy of the license can be viewed at http://www.nisyndication.com/terms.html

Figure 1 on page 68 is reproduced with the permission of Guardian News & Media Ltd, *Copyright Guardian News & Media Ltd 2002*.

The following images are licensed under the GNU Free Documentation License. Permission is granted to copy, distribute and/ or modify this document under the terms of the GNU Free Documentation License, Version 1.2 or any later version published by the Free Software Foundation; with no Invariant Sections, no Front-Cover Texts, and no Back-Cover Texts. A copy of the license can be viewed at http://www.gnu.org/licenses/fdl.html

Pages 10, 30 (top), 45 (top right), 45 (top left), 45 (bottom left), 55, 69 (bottom), 73 (right)

The following images are licensed under the Creative Commons Attribution 3.0 Unported License. Permission is granted to share and/or remix this work providing the work is attributed in the manner specified by the author or licensor. A copy of this license can be viewed at http://creativecommons.org/licenses/by-sa/3.0/deed.en

Cover (top and bottom), pages 10, 30 (top), 34 (bottom), 45 (top right), 45 (top left), 45 (bottom left), 66, 69 (bottom), 73 (right)

### Picture credits

All photographs are by the authors except for the following which are included with kind permission of the copyright holders:

Alvesgaspar: 45 (top right)
Asterion: 34 (bottom)
Behn Lieu Song: 45 (top left)
Chris McKenna: 30 (top)
Dan Lundenberg: 66
iStockphoto: cover (middle two), 13, 49, 50, 51, 54, 56, 58 (top left), 63, 64, 65, 67
Jason Minshull: 15
Jerry Strzelecki: 69 (bottom)
Kallerna: 36

Matt Lever: 45 (bottom left)
Marksie531: 73 (right)
Martin Olsson: 45 (top middle)
Nathan Dixey: 69 (top)
P177: cover (bottom)
Sarah Newberry: 45 (bottom right)
Simon Ledingham: 23
Stephan Kühn: cover (top), 10
Steven Royle: 58, 60
US Department of Defense: 24, 25 (top)
US Department of Energy: 25 (bottom), 26
US Navy: 12
Wesley Johnston: 36